THE NON-EXISTENCE OF GOD

THE
NON-EXISTENCE
OF GOD

LINGUISTIC PARADOX IN TILLICH'S THOUGHT

Robert R. N. Ross

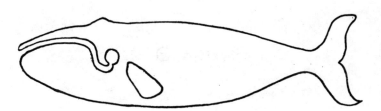

THE EDWIN MELLEN PRESS
NEW YORK AND TORONTO

THE NON-EXISTENCE OF GOD

LINGUISTIC PARADOX IN

TILLICH'S THOUGHT

by

Robert R. N. Ross

Library of Congress Cataloging Number 78-65486

Printed in the United States of America

For

Dr. Milton R. Ross

and

Nancy Newberry Ross

CONTENTS

I wish to thank the editors of the
Harvard Theological Review and the *International Journal for Philosophy of Religion*
for permission to use material from articles
published, by the author, in those journals
in chapters one through three of this book.

I am also appreciative of a faculty
research grant from Skidmore College which
assisted in the completion of this manuscript.

R. R.

INTRODUCTION

The essays of this book comprise a series of
investigations which were begun in 1973 and termi-
nated, at least for the time being, in the summer
of 1978. The subject of the investigations is a
certain class of theological claims about God
which have the paradoxical consequence of prohibiting some important affirmation of God. Tillich's
claim that "God does not exist" is an example of a
paradox of this sort.

While the essays do, I feel, bring to a conclusion a number of specific problems, it would be
foolish to regard dilemmas that are at least as old
as Plato's theory of Ideas as in any way permanent-
ly "settled." Like the phoenix, the kind of paradox which often seems to be intrinsic to the concept of God (or concepts in significant respects
analogous to God, like Platonic Ideas) has a way of
rising once again in other forms. Parmenides of
Elea displayed what is perhaps the paradigm for
this paradox when he argued that a world of seeming
plurality is ultimately One——a single unit. But I,
in a sense, experience another form of this paradox
when I contemplate the simultaneity of the isola-
tion of my individuality and my solidarity with the
species. The latter instance should at least make

it clear that these paradoxes are not simply about formal matters.

Apart from an obvious need to explicate and clarify certain difficult areas in Tillich's theological writings, the primary purpose of these essays is, as I have suggested, to examine a perplexing set of related problems Tillich's theology exemplifies. It is worth noting that these are paradoxical claims about God's nature which arise out of theological analyses of that concept. That is, what the claims have in common is the anomaly that a certain theological analysis of the concept of God apparently results in a significant denial of God, rather than the denial deriving from any philosophical critique. The confusion is compounded, however, because from the theological standpoint, this denial turns out not to be a "denial" at all, but, rather, the only possible way of affirming the reality of God. This is surely the case for Tillich, whose denial that God exists is a direct result of the one positive assertion about God he feels can be literally made: viz., that God is being-itself. But that denial, then, cannot mean what it says, and one is thus forced to seek some other interpretation of it. For example: that the "denial" functions as a way of pointing to the paradoxical conditions of affirming God. The problem with paradoxes, however, is that they generate a myriad of possible interpretations in the course of which the paradox gets transferred, perhaps, but never removed.

There are, roughly, two levels at which such equivocal looking denials of God have been made. Most typically, what has been denied is something about us: i.e., that we can be in a position to know anything about God. Thus, for example, from the doctrine that God is his own being, Aquinas concludes it must be the case that God is "beyond all that can be known of him." Classically, and in Aquinas' case, this has not prevented theologians from going on to assert all sorts of things about God. Naturally, however, it has put considerable strain on the status of our "knowledge" in theological claims that *prima facie* look as if they are asserting something we take ourselves to know about God. This surely includes a whole body of dogmatic utterances about God, e.g., "God created the world," "God loves us." It would seem that such utterances cannot be understood to constitute a body of knowledge about God. Hence, it is out of this situation that there arises a serious problem in understanding what theological assertions about God can properly be said to be "about." If Aquinas, in the long run, does allow us a certain kind of "knowledge" of God, then in order to avoid the admission that he has simply contradicted himself, the knowledge of God he grants, as Mascall points out, cannot be in any way of God's essence. But in that case, remarks that look as if they are claims about the divine nature must be about something else: viz., the world or the effects of the divine nature.

Not all of these denials are about what we
can know, however. Many are expressed as denials
of the applicability of certain natural predicates
to the divine nature itself; i.e., the via negativa. God is infinite, immutable, immaterial, etc.
Now while such statements are, as in the first case,
directives to us (i.e., they are theological assertions which take the form of prohibiting some positive assertion: for instance, that we can properly
apply material predicates to God), they are also,
legitimately, claims about God——claims which tell
us what God is not. By themselves, the claims of
negative theology are not immediately paradoxical,
but only become so when put in relation to other
theological assertions about God (e.g., as in the
doctrines of creation, incarnation and the trinity)
which look quite inconsistent with the former. It
is this circumstance which generates what Kierkegaard calls the "absolute paradox"——i.e., that the
infinitely transcendent, external, immaterial God
should be identical with the God that has "come into being, has been born, grown up, and so forth."
It may well be that there is simply no non-paradoxical way to describe the relation between an infinite, transcendent God and the finite world at all,
let alone in terms of the difficulties which arise
from the peculiarly Christian ways of understanding
that relationship. Nevertheless, the paradoxes (or
contradictions) which arise with the via negativa
can at least be seen in terms of the simultaneity
of apparently inconsistent assertions about God,

and not assertions which, theologically as well as philosophically, surely look self-contradictory in themselves.

But it is assertions about God of precisely the latter sort which I want to examine here. These are statements which, by themselves, intuitively look utterly incomprehensible as meaningful assertions about God from any possible standpoint of being made within the circle of faith. Yet curiously, the assertions I have in mind of this latter sort—including Tillich's claim "God does not exist"—are regarded by the theologians who make them as expressions of faith, not a denial of it. One can probably even identify a kind of mini-tradition among whose members are the Pseudo-Dionysius, Kierkegaard and Tillich—theologians who, in one way or another, draw from doctrines asserting God is necessarily above all existing things the conclusion that it may be even better to say God doesn't exist. Yet one wants to know, after all, why a Christian theologian should want to make such a claim.

One might be inclined to explain those claims away as simply the rantings of theologians who already have a propensity towards paradox and mysticism of a certain sort. The problem with that, however, is that, at least in Tillich's case, not only does the statement "God does not exist" follow directly from the one positive assertion he thinks can be made about God ("God is being-itself"), but it is also a result of a philosophico-theological analysis of the concept of God—i.e., a rational

investigation of the meaning of God, not the
mystical view that we can't comprehend that meaning. Moreover, Tillich's analysis, while ultimately, I feel, unsuccessful, is not trivial or obviously misguided. Even if Tillich finally must
be seen as contradicting himself in the statement
"God does not exist," it is (1) exceedingly difficult to show in precisely what that contradiction
lies, (2) a contradiction Tillich is quite willing
to admit anyway, and (3) it is in any event not a
contradiction of a flat or boring kind. Moreover,
why it is neither flat nor boring is, I think, of
considerable religious significance.

Now if this ambiguity is indicative of anything, as I am convinced it is, then what Tillich
sees as a "necessity" for atheistic statements may
very well turn out to be a direct result of features intrinsic to the concept of God. Tillich's
claim for this is interesting in that regard because he surely feels atheism (of his own sort, at
any rate) is a result of an investigation of the
proper meaning of the concept of God. Two problems
arise from this, however. First, it creates the
tendency, in many of Tillich's remarks, to sense
the construction of deliberate paradox. Second,
one wants to know how much of Tillich's "atheism"
results from his use of the particular concept of
"being-itself" as the philosophical explanation of
the religious notion of God. These questions, and
others, will be considered in the course of the essays.

The first essay sets Tillich's claim that
God does not exist in the context of the Pseudo-
Dionysius and Aquinas, and discusses the extent to
which that statement can be taken non-equivocally.
In the second essay, Tillich's concept of being-
itself is examined, with particular reference to
another of Tillich's radical theological positions:
viz., that God is not a being. The third piece
discusses some of the epistemological aspects of
Tillich's concept of being-itself and how Tillich's
analysis of being-itself from this viewpoint leads
to an argument with considerable resemblance to the
ontological argument. Finally, the separate lines
of these issues are tentatively held together for a
time in a general discussion of the nature of theological paradox.

No investigation of this sort can proceed in
the absence of a considerable amount of pain. If a
certain repetitiousness seems to arise at times it
is only, where not a fault of style, because I
think it is important to take seriously the fact
that theologians so often seem to equivocate and
contradict themselves, and that worries about equivocation and contradiction often look circular or
redundant. I suppose I have a bias which assumes
that those Christian theologians who are the most
interesting, both philosophically and religiously,
are the ones who end up with these sorts of problems, because they have consistently resisted more
easily defensible but religiously empty solutions.
But these problems are painful ones, and at times

I know I merely reflect that fact rather than il-
luminate it. Like the reflections of sunlight on
moving waters, the attempt to clarify often cap-
tures only ambiguities. Perhaps it is some con-
solation to think that those born along the edges
of the sea (as I was) are inexorably locked into
a relationship with ambiguity—not because ambiguity is perversely satisfying, but because the
edge of the sea never stays in one place long
enough to be captured.

Robert R. N. Ross
Four-Mile Beach
Wellfleet, Cape Cod
November 4, 1978

THE NON-EXISTENCE OF GOD

CHAPTER ONE

TILLICH, AQUINAS AND THE PSEUDO-DIONYSIUS ON THE NON-EXISTENCE OF GOD

Because the notions of finitude and temporality often get associated with the concept of "existence," theologians have sometimes found cause to worry about what we are doing when we assert the existence of God. Perhaps the most radical expression of this worry occurs in Paul Tillich's *Systematic Theology* where he claims, paradoxically, that "God does not exist."[1] Despite the fact that the remark appears in a book written both within the tradition of, and about, Christian theology, Tillich spends considerable effort trying to convince us why the affirmation that God does exist must be striken from Christian discourse. Tillich tells us, for example, that "however it is defined, the 'existence of God' contradicts the idea of a creative ground of essence and existence."[2] Therefore, "to argue that God exists is to deny him."[3] Not only would it be

---

[1] Paul Tillich, *Systematic Theology* (3 vols., Chicago: University of Chicago Press, 1951-63), I, p. 205. (Hereinafter referred to as, e.g., ST I, p. 205).

[2] ST I, pp. 204-5.

[3] ST I, p. 205.

"a great victory for Christian apologetics if the
words 'God' and 'existence' were very definitely
separated";[4] indeed, theology "must eliminate the
combination of words 'existence' and 'God.'"[5] In
short, "it is as atheistic to affirm the existence
of God as it is to deny it."[6]

While the effect of remarks such as these
gives one reason to wonder just how Tillich could
be doing anything else but some form of a-theology,
I think it is clear this is not Tillich's intention.
The purpose of this chapter, then, will be to show
not only that Tillich is committed to the existence
of God, but indeed that it is Tillich's intention
to affirm one of the important doctrines of classical Christianity. Specifically, it will be argued
that when God is understood to be beyond the distinction between essence and existence, then Tillich
does allow that "exists" can be meaningful applied
to God.

In the course of this chapter reference will be
made to two other representatives of the tradition
in which the worry about asserting God's existence
gets expressed: Aquinas and the Pseudo-Dionysius.
By examining them on this matter I hope to make more
explicit the nature of Tillich's motive behind the
claim "God does not exist," and to suggest that it
would be wrong to interpret this remark as an in-

---

[4] ST I, p. 205.

[5] ST I, p. 206.

[6] ST I, p. 237.

tention to deny there is a God.

i

Tillich was not the first Christian theologian to see that there might arise some semantic necessity for suggesting that God does not "exist." In the *Summa Theologiae* Aquinas notes that the Pseudo-Dionysius also had said God does not exist, that "God...is not there: he is beyond what is there."[7] This remark arises in Aquinas' discussion of the possibility of our knowledge of God, and the question of whether any created mind can see God's essence. According to Aquinas, the purpose of the Pseudo-Dionysius' claim was to describe the situation of the finiteness of the human mind and the limits of possible knowledge of God. Since the human mind can only know "what is already there to be known"[8] and since God is "beyond what is there, ... he is not intelligible, he is beyond understanding."[9] In the *Mystical Theology* the Pseudo-Dionysius refers to our acknowledgement of this circumstance as the "darkness of unknowing," the "divine gloom," in which, after the mind has removed the inadequate and anthropomorphic images from its concept of God,

---

[7]Thomas Aquinas *Summa Theologiae* Ia. A. 12, art. 1, obj. 3 [Blackfriars], referring to Dionysius the Areopagite *Divine Names* IV, 2. See also *Divine Names* V, 1; V, 4.

[8]*Ibid*.

[9]*Ibid*.

it renounces all apprehension of God by the understanding and becomes mystically united to the God
who is wholly unknowable by the finite mind.[10]

Aquinas saw the Pseudo-Dionysius' point, but
felt this way of speaking was dangerous. For while
Aquinas agreed that we cannot in this life know
God's essence, even after the proofs,[11] there is,
all the same, some knowledge of God. Indeed, we do
know and can prove that God exists and that his essence is identical with his existence.[12] Thus, although God's essence is itself beyond our mortal
apprehension, nevertheless, it can be shown that
certain propositions we frame about God are true.
In particular, according to Aquinas, it can be
proven that in the affirmation "God exists" subject
and predicate stand for the same thing. Consequently, Aquinas tried to make the Pseudo-Dionysius'
point in a different way by saying: "God is not
said to be 'not there' in the sense that he does
not exist at all, but because being his own existence he transcends all that is there."[13]

Aquinas clearly acknowledged the infinite

---

[10]Dionysius the Areopagite *Mystical Theology*
I, 3; II, 1; III, 1. When entering into the gloom
which is above the mind, the contemplative finds not
just little speaking but a complete absence of
speech, and absence of conception.

[11]Aquinas *Summa Theologiae* Ia. A. 3, art. 4,
reply 2; Ia. Q. 12, art. 11.

[12]*Ibid.*, Ia. Q. 3, art. 4, reply 2.

[13]*Ibid.*, Ia. Q. 12, art. 1, reply to obj. 3.

distance between the human mind and God. Yet he
did not want to be committed to an absolute dis-
continuity between them. Specifically, Aquinas
wanted not to be forced, as he suspected the Pseudo-
Dionysius was, into having to deny one can have any
knowledge of God at all—into having to claim God
is simply unintelligible. For Aquinas God in himself is infinitely intelligible; it is we who do
not have infinite understanding.[14] But in this position Aquinas believed it was possible to hold
both to the radical difference between God and the
human mind, yet also retain the demonstrability of
some knowledge of God. To do this required proof:
proof that God does exist and that God is his own
being. Nevertheless, knowing that meant that we
could know something about the way in which God
differs from ordinary existing things. It did not,
as it had for the Pseudo-Dionysius, represent the
total absence of knowledge. It was not a void, a
blank, nor was it a mystical union in which rationality was totally renounced.

When God is understood by Aquinas to exist
above all that exists because he is his "own being,"
then it is clear Aquinas is also saying God just
isn't an ordinary existing thing, a "being among
others." Indeed, it is in this sense that Aquinas
recognizes a certain justice to the Pseudo-Dionysius'
claim. For like Aquinas, the Pseudo-Dionysius was
attempting to make the suggestion that it lies in

---

[14]Cf. *Ibid.*, Ia. Q. 12, art. 7, reply to
objs. 2 and 3.

the concept of "God" itself that God is necessarily beyond existence. The Pseudo-Dionysius, however, drew from this the conclusion that, if God
is necessarily "above" all existing things, then
it may even be better to say God doesn't exist.
But the problem with that claim—which Aquinas recognized as going one step further—was that it obviously brought into question the possibility of
there being religious epistemology at all. For no
matter how inscrutable one might believe the nature
of the object of religion must be, it would be absurd to suggest that what we are worshipping is,
after all, something non-actual. Nevertheless, in
setting the limits of any religious epistemology,
Aquinas was aware that part of the logic required
laying out certain claims about God which prohibit
one from understanding God as just another existing
thing "out there" whose nature can be inferred from
these existing things "here." In particular, if it
is a claim about God that God is his "own" being,
then it is analytic that God cannot be thought of
in terms of ordinary existing things, since it is
precisely denied about "things" that they can be
their "own" being. For this reason there can be no
possibility of any inference to God's nature from
ordinary existing things—their natures in this respect are contradictory. Indeed, even before the
proofs Aquinas is careful to warn that while God's
effects can serve to demonstrate that God is, this
does not mean they can help us to know what God

is.[15] The limits of our religious knowledge, then,
are established by virtue of the fact that God's
nature must be conceived of as contrary to our own,
and one expression for this difference has been
the claim that God "transcends" all existence. But
from the notion that God transcends existence, it
does not follow that God is "without" existence,
as the Pseudo-Dionysius had implied. It is at this
point that Aquinas believed the Pseudo-Dionysius to
have fallen into error, and I will want to return
to this matter in the course of my discussion of
Tillich.

For Aquinas there is a sense in which the
only possibility of asserting God's existence depends upon our acknowledgement of the doctrine that
God's essence and existence are identical. Whereas
ordinary existing things exist by virtue of something other than their own essence, it is God's nature to exist. God's nature is primarily to be.[16]
Thus, if it can be proven that God's essence is
identical with his existence, then Aquinas believes
God's existence can be asserted without contradiction, even though it is this very doctrine that establishes the radical difference in nature between
God and created beings, and poses the problem of
asserting God's existence in the first place. For
the notion of a being whose essence and existence

---

[15]*Ibid.*, Ia. Q. 2, art. 2, reply to obj. 3.

[16]It is this claim about God which has traditionally made the acceptance of some version of the
ontological argument look inviting.

are identical with him and with each other is the
notion of a being about which it would be absurd
to say it didn't exist. The doctrine, in short,
is about a being whose existence is in some sense
necessary.

Perhaps even more important, however, is the
fact that it is also from this doctrine that Aquinas draws the conclusion that it is not the case
that God cannot be known; rather, "...he is beyond
all that can be known of him."[17]   From the doctrine
that God's essence and existence are identical,
that is, Aquinas draws both the basis of, and the
conditions for, the possibility of making any intelligible statements about God at all. The doctrine of the identity of God's essence and existence establishes, first of all, an infinite difference in kind between God and ordinary existing
things. Its subject is a being of whose nature we
have no clear apprehension because, unlike ourselves, it is a being whose existence is underiva-
tive. But if it can be shown that the concept of
such a being is not incoherent—if we can know what
is meant by the notions of "essence" and "existence," and also prove that there is a being, God,
who verifies those predicates simultaneously,[18]

---

[17]Aquinas *Summa Theologiae* Ia. Q. 12, art. 1,
reply to obj. 3.

[18]See also, e.g., P. T. Geach, "Commentary on
Aquinas," in Donald R. Burrill, ed., *The Cosmologi-
cal Arguments,* Anchor Book (Garden City: Doubleday
& Company, Inc., 1967), pp. 78-9.

then one can allow for the possibility of making
intelligible statements about such a being.

According to Aquinas, it is not the case that
God is unknowable, or beyond all knowledge, in the
sense that the concept of God is unintelligible.
Even though God is beyond what can be known of him,
assertions using the concept "God" do not involve
one in any immediate contradiction. If it were
true that God was unknowable, simply unknowable,
the implication would be that one ought to stop
talking about there being such a thing as God altogether. However, Aquinas' point is that God's nature transcends the finiteness of the human mind;
or, as the Pseudo-Dionysius sometimes suggested,
the human mind is "rendered blind" by the intensity
of the divine light. Thus, while it is one thing
to say God is beyond knowledge, it is quite another
to say the concept "God" has no place in knowledge
because it is unintelligible. But it was the former, Aquinas argued, that was what the Pseudo-
Dionysius really meant—or ought to have meant—by
saying God "cannot be comprehended."[19]

It would be misleading, however, to suggest
that the Pseudo-Dionysius himself flatly denies
God's existence. God is more often said to be
something not existing but "super-existing." The
transcendent Godhead does not belong to the category of existence, but neither does it belong to

---

[19]Aquinas *Summa Theologiae* Ia. Q. 12, art. 1,
reply to obj. 3.

the category of non-existence.[20] Now at least
once, Tillich also uses the neo-Platonic formula
of "super-existence" in order to explain what he
means by saying that God is "above" existence or
"beyond" existence. According to Tillich, God "is
not an existing thing" not because there is no God,
but because God "is...the Super-existing, that which
is at the same time the absolute Nothing and the
absolute Something."[21] With respect to ordinary
existing substances, God is wholly other—the absolute Nothing (i.e., absolutely "unlike"). But in
the sense that God himself is the creative ground
of all being, the source of being in everything that
is, God is the absolute Something.

It seems reasonable, then, to suggest that
Tillich's claim "God does not exist" expresses fundamentally the same worry as we have seen expressed
by the Pseudo-Dionysius and Aquinas. The question
now before us is: does Tillich's solution to that
problem fundamentally differ from that of Aquinas?

ii

It has been suggested that for Aquinas the

---

[20]Cf. Dionysius the Areopagite *Mystical Theology* V.

[21]Paul Tillich, "Ueber die Idee einer Theo-
logie der Kultur," in *Religionsphilosophie der
Kultur; Zwei Entwürfe von Gustav Radbruch und Paul
Tillich* (Berlin: Reuther und Reichard, 1919), p.
35, quoted in James Luther Adams, *Paul Tillich's
Philosophy of Culture, Science, and Religion* (New
York: Schocken Books, 1970), pp. 43-44.

ability to assert God's existence rests on an acknowledgement of the doctrine that in God essence
and existence are identical because God is his
"own" being. The presupposition of this doctrine
is the implicit condition for asserting God's existence. Does Tillich also hold this? Does Tillich also hold, like Aquinas, that one can assert
God's existence if God's essence and existence are
understood to be identical? I will argue that he
does.

One way this can be brought out involves the
classical distinction between "essence" and "existence" which has been referred to but not yet made
explicit. In general, for any given thing which
is said to exist or have being, one can roughly
mark off a distinction signified by the applicability of two questions: (1) whether a thing exists
(an sit), its "existence" corresponding to what is
asserted by the fact that it is, and (2) what a
thing is (quidditas), what the nature or essence
of a thing is, what kind of thing it is by which
it differs from other species of things. "Existence" is sometimes said to refer to the "act" by
which an individual thing actually has the essence
which is constitutive of its particular form.[22] It
is the act which individuates a thing. "Essence,"
on the other hand, is something there to be referred to whether it exists or not. Essence is
that by which something can be said to be of a

---

[22]Aquinas *Summa Theologiae* Ia. Q. 3, art. 4,
reply to obj. 2, for example.

certain kind and by which it is able to be associated with other things of the same kind.

Now sometimes Tillich implies that to assert
that something exists is to specify that "something" as a member of the class of "the totality of
beings,"[23] from which it follows that it is "subject to the categories of finitude, especially to
space and substance,"[24] or that it is "conditioned"[25]—i.e., dependent on something else for
its existence. In other words, Tillich sometimes
seems to be suggesting that to assert the existence
of something entails that it is a finite, particular being in the sense he calls "a being among others." But if something is a being among others, it
would seem to be subject to the applicability of
the distinction between its essence and its existence—between what it is and the fact that it is.
However, it is not clear how one ought to take this
"entailment." Does Tillich hold that the distinction between essence and existence necessarily follows from the meaning of "exists" alone? Unfortunately it is far from clear just what Tillich believes follows from the concept of "exists." Nevertheless, if, for Tillich, it is analytic or part of
the meaning of "exists" so that to assert the existence of x necessarily means that for every x its essence is distinct from its existence, then clearly

---

[23] ST I, p. 205.

[24] ST I, p. 235.

[25] ST I, p. 173.

Tillich cannot, as Aquinas believed he could, consistently assert the existence of God and also hold
that in God there is no distinction between his essence and existence because God is "beyond" that
distinction (i.e., that God is not a being "among"
others).

But Tillich does hold that in God there is no
distinction between his essence and existence, for
he accepts as true[26] the scholastic doctrine that
"in God there is no difference between essential
and existential being. This implies that the split
[between essence and existence]...has no relevance
for the ground of being itself."[27] God, Tillich
continues, "is not subjected to a conflict between
essence and existing. He is not a being beside
others.... His existence, his standing out of his
essence, is an expression of his essence. Essentially he actualizes himself. He is beyond the split....
God alone is 'perfect,' a word which is exactly defined as being beyond the gap between essential and
existential being."[28]

Consequently, if there is to be any way which
Tillich might allow it as permissible to assert
God's existence, then it would seem Tillich cannot
hold it is analytic, or from the meaning of "exists"
alone that for every *x* its essence is distinct from
its existence. Indeed, Tillich himself never says

---

[26]ST II, p. 23.

[27]ST II, p. 22.

[28]ST II, p. 23.

this distinction is part of the meaning of the
word "exists." Later, we will see that Tillich
associates an idea similar to the distinction between essence and existence—which carries with it
notions of spatial and temporal finitude—with the
term "exists." This, however, does not arise from
a direct inspection of the meaning of exists. For
now let us assume it is only when one asserts the
existence of an x that is what Tillich calls "a
being among others," that it follows its essence
and existence are distinct. One can ask of a being
"among" others both what it is and whether it is.
But since Tillich denies that God is a being "among"
others, he is still in a position, at least in principle, to affirm God's existence without contradiction.

It must be admitted that this seems to go
against some of Tillich's own words—which suggest
that to assert the existence of God is "a contradiction in terms."[29] But in judging that Tillich
means to leave it open that there is a way one can
sensibly affirm God's existence—indeed, that Tillich himself presupposes throughout his entire theology that there is a God—I considered the following.

First, as I have suggested, if Tillich held
that it was analytic, or part of the meaning of the
word "exists," that essence and existence are, for
every x, distinct, then Tillich would have to re-

---

[29]Cf. ST I, p. 207.

gard the doctrine that in God essence and existence
are identical—a doctrine which, as it were, is a
permission to assert God's existence—as either
false or unintelligible. But Tillich does not regard that doctrine as false. He explicitly claims
it as true. Moreover, for Tillich, it does not
seem to be part of the meaning of the word "exists"
that essence and existence are distinct. Thus it
remains open as at least logically possible that
there should be a case for which this distinction
has no application. Therefore, it also remains
possible for Tillich to assert the existence of God
without involving ourselves in "a contradiction in
terms."

Secondly, if Tillich really believed asserting
God's existence were a contradiction, so that from
any use of "exist" it followed that to assert God's
existence were to utter something false or meaningless, then any remark in which the existence of God
were implied or presupposed would also be meaningless. Yet it should be equally obvious that Tillich
is far from drawing the conclusion that there is no
God or that writing theology is meaningless. Indeed,
to the contrary, the abundance of dogmatic claims
about God which Tillich affirms forces one to conclude that his entire theology simply presupposes
the existence of God. What one finds Tillich most
typically saying is that discussions or arguments
about the existence or non-existence of God are
meaningless.[30] This, however, is quite a different

---

[30]Cf. Paul Tillich, *Dynamics of Faith,* Harper
Torchbooks (New York: Harper & Row, 1957), p. 67.

matter, and it may only be a way of indicating
that he finds such arguments pointless, religiously. Thus, even if Tillich does find the question
of the existence of God meaningless, it is in any
case not because he regards the concept of God "unintelligible."

But if the claim that to assert the existence
of God is a "contradiction in terms" does not prohibit Tillich, in his theology, from presupposing
the existence of God, just what, one wants to know,
does Tillich believe to be contradictory about affirming God's existence? In brief, it is the idea
of an argument for the existence of an unconditioned being "within reality."[31] Tillich's assumption here—warranted or otherwise—is that in arguing for God's existence we are somehow forced to
conceive of God as a being within reality where
"within" seems to have the force of meaning "an
individual part of reality," or, perhaps, "the universe" itself. According to Tillich, the God argued for by the "reasoning" used in arguments for
his existence is "less than God"[32] for his nature
is "derived from the world."[33] But this "brings
God's existence down to the level of that of a
stone or a star...."[34] The result is that God be-

---

[31]ST I, p. 207.

[32]ST I, p. 74.

[33]ST I, p. 205.

[34]Paul Tillich, "The Two Types of Philosophy
of Religion," in *Theology of Culture,* ed. by Robert
C. Kimball, A Galaxy Book (New York: Oxford University Press, 1964), p. 18.

comes identified as "a particular being,"[35] "a
being alongside others...something conditioned by
something else which is also conditioned."[36] But
when we "bring him down to the level of a thing in
the world...,[37] the term 'God' becomes interchangeable with the universe and therefore is semantically superfluous."[38] The outcome of Tillich's worry
about what he thinks happens when we speak of God
as "existing" is this: not only does bringing God
"into" the world make it easier to deny his existence;[39] indeed, he says, it "makes atheism...almost
unavoidable."[40]

But why is Tillich worried that our affirming
that God "exists" entails "bringing him into the
world"? Why does Tillich suggest, with an air of
deliberate paradox, that the God who exists "...
ceases to be the God who is really God";[41] he ceases
to be an object of "ultimate concern"?[42] Just what
does this worry mean? It means, for one thing, that

---

[35]ST I, p. 211.

[36]ST I, p. 242.

[37]Paul Tillich, "The Idea of God as Affected
by Modern Knowledge," *Crane Review* Vol. I, No. 3
(spring, 1959), 87.

[38]ST II, p. 7.

[39]Tillich, "The Idea of God as Affected by
Modern Knowledge," p. 87

[40]Tillich, "The Two Types of Philosophy of
Religion," p. 18.

[41]ST I, p. 172.

[42]Cf. ST I, p. 12.

if we were talking about things like stones and
stars when we argue for God's existence, we would
not be talking about God. And, of course, one can
quite agree with Tillich that if all we meant by
"God" were simply a very large and hard-to-get-rid-
of physical object (say, the universe), then God
might just as well be, as Kierkegaard once quipped,
a "tremendously large green bird, with a red beak."[43]
But whether the "ordinary theist"[44]—one, presumably, for whom the arguments for God are at least
relevant to faith—has ever meant by "God" any of
the things Tillich suggests he does is another
story. It may be that certain arguments turn out
that way, although Tillich never shows this. But
that the "ordinary theist" necessarily begins by
thinking of God as such an object (however large or
however hard-to-get-rid-of) is an assumption which
is in need of some justification. Does it follow,
after all that, from the claim "God exists" that
"God" must therefore refer to some finite, conditioned entity in the world (or even to "the entire
world")? It does not seem immediately obvious that
it does.

Since Tillich holds Aquinas' doctrine that
God's essence and existence are identical to be
true, and consequently there is nothing which rules

---

[43] Soren Kierkegaard, *Concluding Unscientific
Postscript,* trans. by David F. Swenson and Walter
Lowrie (Princeton: Princeton University Press, 1941),
p. 219

[44] Cf. ST I, p. 245.

out at least one way for Tillich to be in a position to assert God's existence without contradiction, the question which must now be asked is this:
is there anywhere in Tillich's theology evidence
which suggests Tillich himself allows that there
are conditions under which the concept of "existence" can meaningfully be applied to God, under
which God's existence can be affirmed? The answer
is that there is.

At several points Tillich explicitly indicates
that the concept of existence can be applied to
God.[45] Indeed, as for Aquinas the acknowledgement
of the doctrine that in God essence and existence
are identical is a condition for asserting God's
existence, for Tillich it is also a condition for
asserting God's existence. But the point is that
Tillich explicitly admits that if we acknowledge
this doctrine as true, then we can affirm God's existence. Tillich says this: "If existence in God
is thought of as united with his essence, I could
apply this concept to the divine life."[46]
Further, since Tillich holds it as true that essence and existence "are not separated in God as in
finite beings,"[47] the conclusion that he means to

---

[45]For example, ST II, p. 23; Charles W. Kegley
and Robert W. Bretall, eds., *The Theology of Paul
Tillich,* The Library of Living Theology, Vol. I (New
York: The Macmillan Company, 1956), p. 339

[46]Kegley and Bretall, *op. cit.,* p. 339.

[47]*Ibid.*

allow for us to affirm God's existence seems clear.

I suspect that part of what for Tillich is "half blasphemous" about asserting God's existence is that in doing so we should think of ourselves as asserting an ordinary empirical fact—in the sense in which the methods of an empirical investigation would be relevant to the discovery of that "fact." For if it is part of the concept of God that God cannot be "a being among others," then God cannot be a member of the universe of "things." But if God is not a member of the class of "things," then the methods of empirical investigation are not applicable to the question of his existence.[48] If God exists, it cannot be a "fact" in the same sense in which, e.g., my existence is a fact. As Tillich puts it: "God does not exist factually." It is "in this sense I call the assertion of the existence of God blasphemous."[49] Clearly, however, this qualifies Tillich's claim that "God does not exist" in a rather significant way. For it makes it clear that it is not Tillich's intention to deny there is a God, but rather to reaffirm the classical theological claim that God is not a physical object.[50]

---

[48]Cf. Tillich, "The Idea of God as Affected by Modern Knowledge," p. 85: "...if God is not a being...he is not within the context of finite things which are open to scientific research...."

[49]Kegley and Bretall, *op. cit.*, p. 339.

[50]See, for example, Aquinas *Summa Theologiae* Ia. Q. 3, art. 5, reply to obj. 1: "God does not belong to the category of substance." See also ST I, p. 209 where Tillich affirms this.

Aquinas' doctrine of the identity of God's essence and existence can now be brought into relation with what I believe we have discovered about Tillich's claim "God does not exist." When Aquinas held one could assert the "existence" of God, it presupposed his having denied that the distinction between essence and existence could be applied in the case of God. God exists but he exists as a being infinitely "other" than ordinary existing things. Tillich's denial that God is a being, a being "among others," is his restatement of this doctrine. I suggest, moreover, that Tillich's claim "God does not exist" amounts to a misguided attempt to reinforce this same point.

Seen in a sympathetic light, I think it becomes possible to understand Tillich's claim "God does not exist" not as a denial that there is a God, but to the contrary, as a statement of the radically unique manner by which God does exist—so unique, however, that for Tillich the term "exists" itself has become "inadequate" for the concept of God,[51] in some way suspect. Less sympathetically, though, one can argue that "exists" is a perfectly valid word to express the purported reality of something— be it God or otherwise. Why, for example, does Tillich sometimes associate finite, spatio-temporal connotations with the term "exists,"[52] making it grammatically improper to apply the term to God? For

---

[51] ST I, p. 204.

[52] ST I, pp. 192-3.

it is false that the word "exists" has finite,
spatio temporal connotations. If, say, a winged
horse existed it would indeed be a finite, spatio-
temporal object, but only because "winged horse"
has spatio-temporal connotations, not because "exists" does.[53] When one affirms the existence of
God one is not affirming the existence of a finite
spatio-temporal object. And if the connotation of
spatio-temporal reference is absent (as it is) when
one does affirm God's existence, this is because
God is not a spatio-temporal object, and not because
one is inappropriately using the term "exists." We
could, of course, invent a new word to replace "exists"—or, even worse, as Tillich does, simply assume there is a God while denying he "exists." But
how are we the better for these added confusions?

While suggesting that Tillich's restatement
of Aquinas' position is perhaps "misguided," I do
not, on the other hand, mean to imply it is simply
unintelligible. At least, I think it is possible
to see what Tillich is trying to do. Consider his
claim that God is not a being "among others." The
denial that God is a being "among others" is relevant to asserting God's existence in this sense: it
becomes part of the logic of asserting God's existence that God is at the same time denied to be an
ordinary existing thing whose nature or essence can

---

[53]Cf. Willard Van Orman Quine, "On What There
Is," *From a Logical Point of View*, Harper Torchbooks (2d ed.; New York: Harper & Row, Publishers,
1963), p. 3.

in some sense be referred to whether or not it exists. In the case of God it makes no sense to
speak of God's nature without, at the same time,
referring to it as an existing nature.[54] One can
sensibly assert that something should be an *F* without implying there is or ever was one. But one cannot affirm that it is possible there should be a
God without implying that God must exist, if indeed
there is a God. It is important to note that we
are not here saying anything about whether or not
God does exist. That is, from this claim about the
concept "God" it does not follow that there actually is a God, as some supporters of the ontological
argument have wanted to maintain.[55] It is, however,

---

[54]This is not the same, however, as saying
one can infer God's existence from his nature. That
is a different matter, and, at least for Aquinas, required a proof from God's effects. But when Tillich
adds to this doctrine the claim that one cannot sensibly even raise the question of God's existence, his
position seems suspiciously close to some form of
ontological argument. Tillich, that is, sometimes
appears to regard it as a feature of the concept
"God" itself that it is senseless to think of God as
not existing. Aquinas, however, specifically rejects
the ontological argument, and his "proofs" of God's
existence are themselves evidence that he regards the
question "Is there a being whose nature is to exist?"
as meaningful——one whose answer must take the form of
a demonstration.

[55]See, e.g., Norman Malcolm, "Anselm's Onto-
logical Arguments," *The Philosophical Review* LXIX,
No. 1 (January, 1960), 41-62, reprinted in John H.
Hick and Arthur C. McGill, eds., *The Many-Faced
Argument* (New York: The Macmillan Company, 1967),
pp. 301-321, especially pp. 316-17.

a classical Christian claim about God's unique nature.   It is what one might call a significant
"grammatical" claim about the meaning of "God," because it tells us what kind of concept the concept
"God" is.   It tells us what features about the concept "God" we must accept if we are meaningfully to
use the concept at all, and it is "grammatical" in
the sense that it informs us of the conditions for
our use of this word.

At least this is one possible interpretation
of what is meant by Aquinas' doctrine that in God
there is no distinction between his essence and
his existence because God is his own being.   God
has his being not from something other than himself.   Every being that is some *F*—some kind of
thing—however, is a created being.   It has its
being from something other than itself.   Whether
or not it exists, whether or not there is some *F*
which actually has the form constitutive of its essence is not a consequence of its own nature. Rather, it is a consequence of God's creation.

An individual existing thing—what Aquinas
calls a "substance"—must be of such a nature that
it can possibly exist.   A purported object whose
nature is such that it could not possibly have that
nature (a round square, for example) cannot possibly
exist.   Nevertheless, a substance which is a possible object is not something which can exist of itself.   From the fact that a given nature is one which
can possibly exist, it does not follow that it does
exist nor that it necessarily exists if, in fact,

there actually is one. As Aquinas puts it, the
nature of a substance "is not itself the thing's
existence."[56]

Only God, then, is the being whose nature is
primarily to be. The nature of created substances
is to be *F* or to be *G*, but not essentially to be.
Whether created substances exist is dependent upon
something other than their own nature or essence.
And that upon which everything is dependent for its
existence, according to Aquinas, is God. But
Aquinas also says that God's being is that to which
"no addition" can be made.[57] God, in other words,
is not some kind of thing but is "existence itself."[58]
God's nature is simply to be[59] in the sense that the
divine being is without the addition of any form by
which it can be identified as of a certain type of
thing within the category of substance. "God does
not belong to the category of substance."[60] "God
is not even a prototype within the genus of substance, but the prototype of all being, transcending
all genera."[61]

---

[56]Aquinas *Summa Theologiae* Ia. Q. 3, art. 5,
reply to obj. 1.

[57]*Ibid.*, Ia. Q. 3, art. 6, reply, ref. to Boethius.

[58]*Ibid.*

[59]*Ibid.*, Ia. Q. 3, art. 5, reply.

[60]*Ibid.*, Ia. Q. 3, art. 5, reply to obj. 1,
cf. also ST I, p. 209.

[61]Aquinas *Summa Theologiae* Ia. Q. 3, art. 6,
reply to obj. 2.

Now when Tillich says that God is not a being, it is essentially Aquinas' doctrine that God is utterly simple——the doctrine that God's essence and existence are identical because God "transcends" all genera——which I believe him to have in mind.   Tillich's claim that God is not a being among others reaffirms the classic theological notion that God does not "fall under" the category of substance. God transcends the distinction between essence and existence which otherwise applies to every substance.[62] But if Tillich is fundamentally restating Aquinas' position here, as I believe he is, then in his claim that "God does not exist," certainly Tillich has come to use "exist" in a deliberately ambiguous way.

The notions of spatial and temporal finitude which Tillich at times associates with the meaning of "exists" play on the language of essence and existence (what Tillich calls "essential" and "existential" being).[63]   Nevertheless, Tillich's peculiar use of "exists" seems to develop from what one might call a religious interpretation of the nature of existence, rather than from a direct analysis of the meaning of "essence" and "existence" or of the word "exists" itself.[64]   Generally, when Tillich speaks of

---

[62]Cf. D. MacKenzie Brown, ed., *Ultimate Concern,* Harper Colophon Books (New York: Harper & Row, Publishers, 1965), p. 45.

[63]See, e.g., ST I, p. 202 ff.

[64]It is religious in this sense: what Tillich claims follows from the meaning of "exists" is primarily relevant only to one who accepts, in some sense, the Christian doctrine of creation and fall.

something "existing," this is understood from the
standpoint of a religious interpretation he places
on the creation and fall of existence,[65] from which
it follows that something "existing" is subject to
the "conditions" of existence: namely, the "disrup-
tions" of the fall from essential being to existential estrangement.[66] "Exists" in this sense refers to a particular state of existence, a particular historical condition of existence, one might
say. It is informed from the perspective of the
Christian doctrine of the fall, in which in everything there is an ontological separation from what
Tillich calls essential or "true" being. Tillich's
name for this state is "estrangement," ("The state
of existence is the state of estrangement"[67]), a
term Tillich adopts from Hegel. This state is vari-
ously characterized by Tillich as being one of
blindness, distortion, falling into non-being, self-
destruction, disruption, disintegration, loneliness,
and ambiguity.

---

[65]Cf. ST II, pp. 22-23.

[66]Cf. ST I, pp. 204-5.

[67]ST II, p. 44. In Tillich's theology existential "estrangement" is also regarded, in some
sense, as a consequence of creation: "creation and
the fall coincide.... Actualized creation and
estranged existence are identical." (*Ibid*.) Tillich's point, apparently, is to emphasize the universality of the fall. (Cf. Kegley and Bretall, *op.
cit.*, p. 343.) The ethical difficulties of this
view—that sin is made into an ontological necessity
instead of our personal responsibility—are discussed
in an essay by Reinhold Niebuhr: "Biblical Thought
and Ontological Speculation," (*Ibid.*, pp. 216-27).

But clearly "exists" in this sense does not apply to God, because it is a sense of "exists" which could not apply to God since God does not number among those created beings who participate in the fall.[68] When Tillich denies that God exists because the concept of existence is said to be inadequate for God, it is this special sense of "exists" he has in mind. Moreover the connection between Tillich's claim "God does not exist" and his denial that God is "a being among others" comes clearer. For ultimately Tillich's denial that God "exists" amounts to nothing more than a rejection of the false idea that God could be a finite being—an individual created substance.

Given Tillich's religiously "weighted" sense of "exists" one can see on what basis he is led to make the claim "God does not exist." Yet the cost of the questionable forcefulness gained in making it comes high. In affirming the reality of God there is a confusion—a confusion Aquinas appreciated but sought to avoid. But because the confusion is a genuine one, it cannot be removed, as Tillich thought, by merely attempting to remove the concept of "existence," or by somehow making it inoperative. Thus, in the case of Tillich, and perhaps the Pseudo-Dionysius as well, the price paid for (sometimes) disallowing the possibility of asserting God's existence is that of losing sight of where to focus our

---

[68]Tillich sometimes allows that there is a sense in which God does participate in the results of the fall (Cf. ST I, pp. 245, 270). But even so, it is not as a created being.

confusion. Ultimately, I believe, Tillich has reduced what is a real problem to one of semantics.
For if the concept of God is intelligible—as Tillich certainly maintains—then the problem is not
that of whether we can say verbally God "exists."
Rather, the problem lies in what follows, religiously, from the fact that we do.

Indeed, it is hard to imagine what it would
even be like to hold on to religion while giving up
all possibility of affirming the existence of God.
Tillich is not, however, any more than Aquinas, suggesting we give up religion. Yet for Tillich it
seems a more crucial question than for Aquinas just
how it can be maintained that religion is the ultimate subject matter of theology. I can only suggest that the confusion in asserting God's existence
should for Tillich, more than it does, be cause for
us to look at what follows in terms of religious
belief: i.e., from acknowledging our inability to
make it known how God is living even though his
life is qualitatively different from creaturely
existence.[69] The solution Tillich sometimes pro-
poses to this dilemma—to simply give up asserting
God's existence—is wrong. And the fact that he
assumes all along the existence of that which he
claims we must deny only prolongs the discomfort.

iii

Tillich attaches to the claim "God does not

---

[69] Cf. ST I, p. 277.

exist"——apparently as an explanation for it——the
statement that God is "beyond essence and existence."[70] Unfortunately this statement has the
tendency to add to the feeling that Tillich commits
himself to some form of atheism. The remark is semantically unclear because it gives the impression
that Tillich means to suggest not merely, in the
manner of Aquinas, that God is beyond the distinction between essence and existence because in him
they are identical,[71] but that God is "beyond" existence altogether. Now to say that God is beyond
the distinction between essence and existence is one
thing. But to say that God is beyond essence and
existence *simpliciter* is quite another. For from
the latter, though not the former, it can only follow that there is no God.

But it is merely an impression that Tillich
is suggesting the latter, however. Tillich himself
later qualifies the remark when, in a reply to one
of his critics, he emphasizes that "the phrase 'beyond essence and existence' does not mean *without*
it."[72] Indeed, Tillich tells us that "there is of
course that being which is beyond essence and existence, which, in the tradition of the classical theology of all centuries, we call God——or, if you pre-

---

[70]Cf. ST I, p. 205.

[71]Cf. Aquinas *Summa Theologiae* Ia. Q. 3, art.
3 and 4.

[72]Kegley and Bretall, *op. cit.*, p. 347, Tillich's emphasis.

fer, 'being-itself'..."[73]

Tillich can hardly be taken to be denying
there is a God here. What he is denying, rather,
is only a "false" construction put on the concept
of God by which God turns out to be nothing more
than a finite entity, characterized by the distinction between what it is and the fact that it is.
Moreover, according to Tillich, to deny that God is
finite is precisely the purpose of the phrase "beyond essence and existence": namely, that God "does
not merely exist and is not merely essential but
transcends that differentiation, which otherwise
belongs to everything finite."[74]

The confusion generated by Tillich's expression "beyond essence and existence," then, is largely verbal and can be removed in the following way.
"Beyond essence and existence," taken literally, appears to be a straight claim about God—one quite
different from the claim that would be made by saying it is part of the concept "God" that God is beyond the differentiation between essence and existence. The latter claim is a "grammatical" remark
about what can and can't be said about God, given
the currency of the concepts "essence" and "existence": to say of God "there is a distinction between
his nature and his existing" does not make sense.
The unclarity of the former claim, however, derives
from the fact that it reads like a negative exist-

---

[73]Brown, *op. cit.*, p. 45.

[74]*Ibid.*, p. 45.

ential. That is, if God is "beyond" existence—
one might so interpret—then it follows that he
does not exist, that there is no God. But when
Tillich tells us that in the phrase "beyond essence
and existence" "beyond" is not meant to imply without existence, that interpretation must be ruled
out. Thus, it is some sense of "beyond" which does
not mean "as if without" that Tillich has in mind.

For Tillich to say God is "beyond" existence
is not to imply that God is a being who has in some
way "outgrown" existence. Rather, it suggests a
certain sense in which Tillich has outgrown the
concept of existence—or in which it has outgrown
him—for it no longer has a clear or unambiguous
use for him. Nevertheless, it remains that by "beyond essence and existence" Tillich does not mean
something fundamentally different from what Aquinas
meant by saying that in God essence and existence
are identical, where the implication is that God is
"beyond" that contrast. Indeed, Tillich himself
sometimes puts it just that way: "As being-itself
God is beyond the contrast of essential and existential being."[75] Despite appearances, then, Tillich
and Aquinas are fundamentally in accord in asserting
God's existence.

iv

For all of Tillich's apparent "atheism" and
for all of Tillich's complaints about the conceptual

---

[75]St I, p. 236.

incompatibility of "God" and "existence," it thus
seems clear that Tillich is by no means intending
to deny there is a God. While affirming that "God
exists" may be theologically unsatisfying to Tillich,
all the same, it does not follow that Tillich regards the statement "God does not exist" as true.

Indeed, when Tillich tells us that "of course"
there is that being which we call God, one suspects
that for Tillich the idea that there might not be a
God is literally inconceivable, and that the existence of God is simply the presupposition of Tillich's
entire theology. For how could it be "conceivable"
when it is said by Tillich that God is the "presupposition" of any question of God,[76] or that the object of religion "can never itself be the object of
doubt,"[77] or, finally, that the very basis of man's

---

[76]Tillich, "The Two Types of Philosophy of Religion," pp. 13, 16. With this remark Tillich is
not simply saying, as one commentator suggests, that
"questions about God, if they are meaningful, must
have their place in the language of a community in
which the word 'God' has a meaningful use." (Edward
CEll, *Language, Existence, and God* (Nashville: Abingdon Press, 1971), p. 48. That is, Tillich is not
simply saying that (knowing the meaning of) the word
"God" is the presupposition of the question of God.
Rather, Tillich is asserting a much stronger thesis:
namely, that the reality of God is a presupposition
of that question. This is perhaps brought out more
clearly elsewhere when Tillich says "an awareness of
God is present in the question of God. This awareness precedes the question." (ST I, p. 206.)

[77]Paul Tillich, "The Philosophy of Religion,"
in *What Is Religion,* ed. by James Luther Adams (New
York: Harper & Row, Publishers, 1969), p. 71.

being is "the God Whom he cannot flee..."[78] because "in every creature God is...more present than the creature is to himself..."[79]

Tillich makes the statement: "The scholastics were right when they asserted that in God there is no difference between essence and existence. But they perverted their insight when in spite of this assertion they spoke of the existence of God and tried to argue in favor of it."[80] Just what, however, is it that Tillich thinks is perverse? I suggest it is this. If God, for Tillich, is something of which we must already be aware because, as being-itself, he is the "presupposition" of any possible question of his existence, then clearly to argue for his existence is not only perverse—indeed it is meaningless. But it is just this point—that discussion of the question of God's existence is meaningless—which Tillich often couples with his claim that God cannot be said to "exist." One finds Tillich saying, for example, that "the question of the existence of God can neither be asked nor answered. If it is asked...the answer—whether negative or affirmative—implicitly denies the nature

---

[78]Paul Tillich, "Escape from God," *The Shaking of the Foundations* (New York: Charles Scribner's Sons, 1948), p. 47.

[79]*Ibid.*, p. 44. Tillich is referring to Martin Luther here. See also Paul Tillich, "God's Pursuit of Man," *The Eternal Now* (London: SCM Press, 1963), pp. 85-93 where Tillich speaks of "being arrested" by God.

[80]ST I, p. 205.

of God."[81]   Or again, "the discussions about the
existence or non-existence [are] meaningless."[82]

What Tillich's claim that God's existence
cannot be discussed amounts to is an attempt to
separate the possibility of raising theological
questions about God from the necessity of having to
construct arguments for his existence. Yet there
is more to this than simply the idea, also suggested by Aquinas, that we can (and must) know what the
word "God" means before any attempt to prove his
existence.[83]   Tillich insists that "the method of
arguing through a conclusion...contradicts the idea
of God"[84] because, in Tillich's mind, once one even
raises the question of God—viz., even a question
about the meaning of the concept "God"—then the
question of God's existence has, *a priori,* already
been settled.

How does this come about? Suppose we examine
why Tillich takes the position of denying that the
arguments for God's existence are really "arguments"
after all. According to Tillich: "The arguments for
the existence of God neither are arguments nor are
they proof of the existence of God."[85]   They are not

---

[81]ST I, p. 237.

[82]Tillich, *Dynamics of Faith,* p. 46.

[83]Aquinas *Summa Theologiae* Ia. Q. 2, art. 2,
reply to obj. 2; also Ia. Q. 13, art. 8, reply, where
Aquinas says that everyone who uses the word "God"
has in mind a certain understanding of what the word
means.

[84]ST I, p. 205.

[85]*Ibid.*

arguments, Tillich continues, because "they are
expressions of the question of God which is implied
in human finitude. This question is their truth;
every answer they give is untrue. This is the
sense in which theology must deal with these arguments, which are the solid body of any natural theology. It must deprive them of their argumentative
character..."[86] Why does Tillich attach such significance to our being able to raise the "question"
of God? In brief, the fact that the "question" of
God should arise in our experience is significant
because it reveals that we are already responsive
to that which we are asking after. It reveals that
we are already responsive to God, who, as being-
itself, is the object of our ultimate concern.

     Tillich's analysis of what a question is in-
vites certain comparisons with Heidegger which are
useful. For both Heidegger and Tillich the question
of "being" (for Tillich this is identical with "the
question of God") is not just asking about something.
It is also asking after (seeking) something because
one is concerned with it. Heidegger makes the remark that "every asking is an asking after,"[87] the
point being that something that is asked "after" is
an issue for us. It is a matter of concern for us.
For Tillich, of course, the question of God is a
question of our "ultimate concern."

---

[86]ST I, pp. 205-6.

[87]Martin Heidegger, *Being and Time,* trans. by
John Macquarrie and Edward Robinson (New York: Harper
& Row, Publishers, 1962), p. 24.

Heidegger begins with an analysis of *Dasein*, the entity we are. According to Heidegger,[88] we are ontically distinctive in that we are "ontological." That is, we already possess some interpretation of being, we are responsive to being. Thus, if we can find out what we are responsive to, we find out what being-itself, the object of our concern, is. Tillich also begins with an analysis of ourselves and tells us that "man is the being who is able to ask questions."[89] Similarly, for Tillich, if we can know what is at issue for man, we will discover what God (being-itself) is. To this end Tillich invites us to "think...what it means to ask a question."[90] Tillich's answer is worth quoting at length:

> It implies...that we do not have that for which we ask. If we had it, we would not ask for it. But, in order to be able to ask for something, we must have it partially; otherwise it could not be the object of a question. He who asks has and has not at the same time. If man is that being who asks the question of being, he has and has not the being for which he asks. Certainly we belong to being—its power is in us—otherwise we would not be. But we are also separated from it; we do not possess it fully. Our power of being is limited.... This is precisely what is meant when we say that we are

---

[88]*Ibid.*, p. 32.

[89]Paul Tillich, *Biblical Religion and the Search for Ultimate Reality,* Phoenix Books (Chicago: The University of Chicago Press, 1955), p. 11. Indeed, "...man...cannot avoid asking, because he belongs to the power of being..." (*Ibid.*, p. 12.)

[90]*Ibid.*, p. 11.

> finite.... But man can and must ask; he
> cannot avoid asking, because he belongs to
> the power of being from which he is separated,
> and he knows both that he belongs to it and
> that he is separated from it.[91]

For Tillich, "being-itself" just is what we discover to be of ultimate concern for ourselves. On the other hand, we also learn what we are—what man is— when we know what is of ultimate concern for us. This circularity[92] is important, because for Tillich (as for Heidegger) the first step in any ontological inquiry is to remember what has "passed into forgetfulness"—i.e., to remember what has become hidden from ourselves. In the case of Tillich, we must remember that what is at stake for us is also the question of being-itself, the question of God. But this can only mean, according to Tillich, that we are already moved, stirred, by our ultimate concern. It means that we already in part "belong," as Tillich puts it, to God—to the "power of being" from which we are estranged, but which, nevertheless, is also already present in us.

It is in this way, I believe, that Tillich regards our having raised the question of God as already, in a sense, settling the matter of his reality. For once we become aware of the fact that the question of the nature of God, who is being-itself, is ontologically bound up with the question of the

---

[91] *Ibid.*, pp. 11-12.

[92] Note, for example, that Tillich employs the same term "power of being" to refer both to God and to the power of being in us.

nature of ourselves, then we see that God is that
being the reality of which it is impossible not to
be aware, even though we cannot fully comprehend
his nature. The task of ontological inquiry is to
bring this awareness out of its "hiddenness." But
it cannot be to establish the reality of that after
which we seek. For its reality—the reality of
being-itself—has already been established by the
fact of our "seeking." Once we can get ourselves
to the point of framing the ontological question—
What is being-itself?—we have reached the point of
awareness of that which is the presupposition of
our having been able to raise the question at all.[93]

This must be part of what motivates Tillich's
perplexing statement: "The question of God is possible because an awareness of God is present in the
question of God. This awareness precedes the question. It is not the result of the argument but its
presupposition."[94] When we come to ask the question
which is of "ultimate concern" to us—a question
Tillich claims we cannot avoid asking—what we discover is that we already in part "have" that which
we are asking after. For the subject of the awareness which "precedes" the question—making the question possible—is precisely the God to whom we are
already responsive.

But if this is true, then it becomes clear
that Tillich's remark "God does not exist" must

---

[93]Cf. ST I, p. 163.

[94]ST I, p. 206.

be regarded as entirely gratuitous. Far from saying what it appears to say, it only masks the sense
in which the existence of God is the underlying assumption of Tillich's entire theology. But what is
perhaps even more disturbing is the ease by which
Tillich moves from denying the applicability of the
concept of existence to God to ruling out as meaningless the possibility of discussing the question
of God's existence at all. Insofar as Tillich's
suggestion that the concept of existence is inadequate for God becomes a move to heighten our awareness of God's otherness, then at least one can ap-
preciate Tillich's intention, if not his execution.
However, when the move begins to look more like an
attempt to simply eliminate any possibility of in-
telligibly discussing the question of God's existence at all, then the situation looks more ominous.

When Tillich tells us that an awareness of
God precedes any question of his existence[95] what
this means, I suggest, is that with respect to the
question of whether there is a God, Tillich regards
the question as meaningless only because he has already begged the question. That is, one cannot
sensibly raise the question of God's existence because of the assumption by Tillich that it is a
necessary feature of any concept of God that we
should always have an awareness of God. But since
this awareness, as Tillich says, always "precedes"
any question of God's existence, the question of
whether God exists is rendered "meaningless" only

[95] ST I, p. 206.

because Tillich has assumed there is just one possible answer to it even before it is asked.

It might be said, then, that Tillich is offering some form of argument which runs: If one properly understands the concept "God" as meaning "that
being which is always present in human awareness,"
then it is senseless to raise the question of God's
existence because it is senseless to raise such a
question about that of which it is impossible not
to be aware. That Tillich does mean to be doing
something like this is perhaps most explicit in an
early work where he says:

> It is meaningless to ask...whether the Uncon-
> ditional "exists,".... For the question
> whether the Unconditional exists presupposes
> already...that which exists unconditionally.
> The certainty of the Unconditional is the
> grounding certainty from which all doubt can
> proceed, but it can never itself be the ob-
> ject of doubt. Therefore the object of re-
> ligion is not only real, but is also the pre-
> supposition of every affirmation of reality.[96]

Tillich has built into his concept of God the necessity of our awareness of God, and it is as a result
of this that he regards it as senseless to raise the
question of God's existence.

Tillich, however, has not shown the question
of God's existence to be meaningless, nor does anything he says about how we must conceive the nature
of God make it meaningless. Given a concept of God
from which it necessarily follows that one cannot
"escape" the awareness of God's presence in his life,

---

[96]Tillich, "The Philosophy of Religion,", p. 71.

one can see the force of the suggestion that the
existence of God cannot be discussed. Yet it is,
I believe, still an intelligible response to say
(or simply admit) that one just does not share any
such awareness——that one does not have it.

Moreover, while one may grant that, if there
is a God, it may be necessary that one should have
awareness of him, one can still raise the question: "But is there such a God?" For it is a
rule of logic that from (x) $(Fx{\rightarrow}Gx)$ one cannot infer $(\exists x)$ (Fx).[97] That is, from "If something is
God, then God is that of which one must be aware"
it does not follow that there is a God of whom we
must be aware. Tillich's making the necessity of
our awareness of God a property of God, as it
were, does not alter the basic problem that has
been thought to render such an argument invalid——
namely, that one cannot infer the fact of something's existence from any property intrinsic to
its concept.

In Tillich's case, I believe, discussions of
God's existence turn out to be pointless, because
he has reduced the situation to that in which one
can only deny he has an awareness another claims.
There is, in other words, no "room" for discussion.
For ultimately, it is not the question of whether
God exists that is unintelligible, but rather the

---

[97]See, e.g., G. E. M. Anscombe, *An Introduction to Wittgenstein's Tractatus*, Harper Torchbooks (2d ed., revised; New York: Harper & Row,
Publishers, 1959), p. 15.

circumstances under which Tillich thinks that discussion must take place. The discussion is pointless, because in Tillich's presentation of the issue it turns out that there is no room for one who
acknowledges God's presence and one who denies it
to differ with each other—to have any basis on
which to differ. By reducing the question of God's
existence to the situation where one can only deny
he has an awareness of something another claims he
must have, the two parties will simply be unintelligible to each other.

　　There is one aspect of Tillich's claim that
we cannot discuss the existence of God—as if we
were discussing the existence of some finite object—
that seems right and even useful, insofar as it is
true that people actually do believe God is an infinitely superior but ultimately finite thing. It
is right insofar as people do confuse belief in God
with idolatry and treat God as "a partner with whom
one collaborates or as a superior power whom one in-
fluences by rites and prayers."[98] That would be an
"insult to the divine holiness"[99] for one would not
be believing in God if one believed that. One would
be believing in "a nothing." On the other hand,
Tillich's claim that God's existence cannot be "discussed" also derives from a position which, while it
denies the possibility of constructing any argument
for God's existence, at the same time, constantly

---

[98] ST I, p. 272.

[99] *Ibid.*, pp. 271-2.

makes theological assertions which presuppose it.
Yet this position, I suggest, clearly weakens the
apologetic task Tillich sees himself as trying to
fulfill. The question "Is there a God?" is intelligible because both answers to it are intelligible.
Furthermore, both answers are intelligible whether
one shares another's awareness or not.

Tillich has not given us any independent argument showing how the awareness of God must be shared.
Nevertheless, it is clear that Tillich believes that
a religious awareness of God is in some way intrinsic to every member of the human species. Tillich
says, for example that even though it may not be our
intention to have this religious awareness, "there
is no consciousness unreligious in substance....
Every act of self-apprehension contains, as its
foundation within reality, the relation to the Unconditional.... Objectively considered, all consciousness is related to God..."[100] But if an awareness of God is in some way intrinsic to everyone,
then all the Christian apologist need do is to point
out to the unbeliever what he has possessed all
along.

Certainly Tillich's own praise for the value
of "atheism"[101] suggests he is unable to see it as a

---

[100]Paul Tillich, "The Conquest of the Concept
of Religion in the Philosophy of Religion," in *What
Is Religion?,* ed. by James Luther Adams (New York:
Harper & Row, Publishers, 1969), pp. 139-40. See
also pp. 126-7.

[101]"It is the religious function of atheism

position from which one could deny what he wants to
claim. In short, for Tillich there can simply be
no atheism, as it is generally understood. What is
substituted for it, by implication, is the notion
that in a curious way "disbelief" is identical with
"inhumanity." Precisely for this reason, however,
Tillich's tendency to regard religious awareness of
God as somehow intrinsic to every member of the
human race has the effect of merely insulating the
question of God's existence from criticism. But the
attempt to insulate the question of God's existence
from criticism in this way is wrong. For the answer
which denies there is a God (as well as that which
affirms it) is an intelligible position even within
religious discourse, and when someone stops believing
in God, it may not be because he has just not understood the concept of God "correctly."

---

ever to remind us that the religious act has to do
with the unconditioned transcendent, and that the
representations of the Unconditioned are not objects
concerning whose 'existence' or 'non-existence' a
discussion would be possible." Paul Tillich, *Re-*
ligiose Verwirklichung (Berlin: Furche, 1929), p.
102, quoted in James Luther Adams, *Paul Tillich's*
Philosophy of Culture, Science, and Religion, p.
247.

CHAPTER TWO

GOD AND SINGULAR EXISTENCE

Theologians have often claimed we are in error in our understanding of the concept of God. But few theologians have thought our misunderstanding so radical as that suggested by Tillich. What Tillich challenges, in his *Systematic Theology,* is the traditional notion of Western theism that God is a unique, singular existing individual. As Tillich puts it, "God is being-itself, not a being."[1]

Is Tillich's claim that God is not a singular being meaningful? Clearly, to see how it can be, we need to know whether Tillich's statement "God is being-itself" is meaningful, since apparently it is the truth of that statement which entails that "God is a being" is false.

I will argue that there is an important sense in which Tillich's explication of "being-itself" cannot be made intelligible. Furthermore, it will be shown that Tillich himself often treats "being-itself" as a singular existing individual—precisely that, in other words, which he wishes to deny God is. For these reasons I will conclude that Tillich's denial that God is a being must be re-

---

[1]ST I, p. 237. See also ST I, p. 163.

garded as gratuitous, and that there is retained
in Tillich's theology a distinct sense in which
God is understood as a singular individual.

                            i

[1]   The argument Tillich gives for denying that
God can be a being is essentially this. If something is a being, then according to Tillich, it is
a member of the class of "the totality of beings."[2]
But something which is a member of that class is
subject to "the categories of finitude."[3] Therefore, it follows that if something is a being, it
must be a finite being.

When Tillich considers something as "subject
to the categories of finitude" he means, at least,
that it exists as an object with physical extension
and location in space. God, of course, is not a
physical object; nor is he finite, for consistent
with classical theology, Tillich agrees that God
transcends the categories under which physical objects fall. That is, God transcends "the world."
Thus, Tillich reasons, if we refer to God as a
being, we have made the mistake of thinking him to
be some perhaps unique but nonetheless ultimately
finite object.

Tillich's argument rests on the equivalence
he sets up between "a being" and membership in the

-----

[2]ST I, p. 205.

[3]ST I, p. 235: "If God is *a* being, he is subject to the categories of finitude, especially to
space and substance."

class of the "totality of beings," from the latter of
which is entailed the logically necessary finitude
of anything that is "a being." Unfortunately,
Tillich's reasons why membership in the class of
"the totality of beings" necessarily entails that
each and every member of that class must be a finite being remain somewhat obscure. Traditionally,
of course, it has been thought possible to include
God as a member of that class and still deny his
finitude by claiming him to be a unique member.
For Tillich, however, this is quite impossible.

While the following certainly does not explain Tillich's reasoning, it does, I think, indicate the kind of worry he has in mind. If something
is a member of the class of the totality of beings
and, by definition, falls under the categories of
space and substance, Tillich believes this means
that its existence becomes a matter for empirical
investigation. In the case of "God," however, this
is impossible. The existence of God, Tillich argues, is not "within the context of finite things
which are open to scientific research."[4] Since
God does not fall under those categories applicable
to physical objects, to think one might investigate
his existence empirically is simply to commit a form
of category mistake. That is, when Tillich says

---

[4]Tillich, "The Idea of God as Affected by
Modern Knowledge," 85. Cf. also *Biblical Religion and
the Search for Ultimate Reality, p. 82.*

"God has never been found"[5] among those objects which "exist," he is meaning not that we've looked around and failed, but rather that it is inconceivable, given a proper understanding of the concept "God," that we should do such a thing as conduct an empirical investigation to determine his existence. Tillich's conclusion, therefore, is that such "confusions in the doctrine of God...could be avoided if God were understood first of all as being-itself."[6] For "God transcends every being and also the totality of beings—the world."[7]

The problem of referring to God as a being, then, is Tillich's belief that in so doing we must identify God as we would a finite, spatio-temporal object. But then the criteria for his existence are the physicist's criteria, which is absurd since God transcends the world. Hence, God cannot be a being.

[2] Tillich's solution to this problem in divine reference is the suggestion that we think of God as a being but as "being-itself." For if God is identified with "being-itself" then we can refer to God in such a way that he does not become subject to the categories of finitude. There are substantial difficulties, however which lie in Tillich's account of what "being-itself" is.

---

[5] "The Idea of God as Affected by Modern Knowledge," 85. Cf. also p. 86.

[6] ST I, p. 235.

[7] ST I, p. 237.

Tillich characterizes his theology as an analysis of what he somewhat loosely terms "the question of God." Now what this analysis leads to is something we may call "'being-itself' or 'power of being' or 'ultimate concern' (in the sense of that about which one is ultimately concerned)."[8] That is, Tillich regards the terms "God," "being-itself," "power of being," etc. as interchangeable.[9] But, Tillich continues, "such names are not the names of *a* being but of a *quality* of being."[10] That is, they are not, strictly speaking, "names" at all but descriptions which constitute a single attribute of something. However, what they are an attribute of turns out to be "everything that is."[11]

By his account of "being-itself," Tillich evidently means to suggest that "being-itself" is in some sense a property of everything. "Being-itself" is the most universal and fundamental predicate, part of the nature of everything. However, if being-itself is not a being but that which is "common to all,"[12] and God is being-itself, then God must be

---

[8] Paul Tillich, "The Meaning and Justification of Religious Symbols," in Sidney Hook, ed., *Religious Experience and Truth* (New York: New York University Press, 1961), p. 7.

[9] Cf. also ST I, pp. 235-6.

[10] Tillich, "The Meaning and Justification of Religious Symbols," p. 7.

[11] *Ibid*.

[12] Tillich, "The Two Types of Philosophy of Religion," p. 13.

that which is "common to all." Thus, if Tillich's concept of being-itself makes sense, then it must make sense to think that God could be a quality or property common to everything. I will return to this later.

As I have indicated, the term "being" is used by Tillich as a predicable term, and in the expression "God is being-itself" it is used that way. "Being-itself" is the predicate "being" applied to God not in the concrete but in its abstract form. Furthermore, Tillich argues, "being-itself" is the one predicate that can be applied to God which literally tells us what the nature of God is.[13] At the same time, this unusual predicate is unlike other, ordinary predicates (such as "...is wise" or "...is blue") in one important respect. It is absolutely unrestricted in its range of applicability. For Tillich, "being"is not simply an attribute of God; it is an attribute of "everything that is." Unlike even very general predicates such as "...is alive" or "...is an animal," which can still sensibly be applied only to certain classes of things, "being" has no such limitation of entities to which it can be meaningfully applied. Indeed, it must be applied to everything, Tillich maintains, because it is only in virtue of something's participation in "being" that we can entertain a thought of it at all. "Being" is "something which is always thought implicitly, and sometimes explicitly, if something

---

[13]Cf. ST I, p. 239.

is said to be."[14] Thus, everything there is must
exemplify the property of which the term "being"—
the same being as that in the predicate "being-
itself"—is in some sense an appropriate descrip-
tion.

Exactly what the term "being" describes is a
matter which Tillich has some degree of difficulty
in making explicit. But there are two features in
his account of this common attribute of everything
which seem clear enough. First, "being" is utterly universal. When, for example, Tillich refers to
it as the "power of being in everything that has
being"[15] he is claiming the existence of some quality which must be universally shared. Second,
"being" is in some way the most basic predicate,
part of everything's intrinsic nature. As Tillich
puts it, "being" is "the power inherent in everything."[16] For these two reasons Tillich sometimes
refers to "being" as "the basic *transcendentale*."

It remains to be seen how this universal
predicate can be informative in making some literal
determination about the nature of God—if indeed
the predicate can be regarded as informative at all.
For that which everything shares, including God,
must certainly be the sparest, most general property imaginable. In fact, it would seem that some-

---

[14]ST I, p. 163.

[15]*Ibid*.

[16]ST I, p. 236.

thing which is possessed, quite automatically, by everything from, e.g., sand to God himself could not possibly constitute the particular nature of anything.

Tillich explains that the criterion by which something can be said to possess "being" is that a concept can be formed of it: "everything which can be conceptualized must have being."[17] Furthermore, everything which has being must also possess some form: for "there is no being without form."[18] However, the predicate "being" in no way determines what form any concept refers to. It does not tell us what kind of thing it is we have conceptualized. It does not tell us, for example, that the "being" we are referring to is the being of an animal or of something blue. Rather, "being," so understood, simply tells us that something has some form or other—that it possesses a certain nature, as yet unspecified, presumably to be specified by some further predicate. The predicate simply tells us, in other words, that it is possible for us to have a certain concept, that a given thing of which we are thinking can sensibly be brought before our consciousness.

How "being" tells us this remains somewhat mysterious. But more important, in the case of "God," where "being" is the only predicate which can have a literal application—i.e., no other

---

[17]ST I, p. 179.

[18]*Ibid*.

predicate is available to make any further determination about God's nature—how "being" tells us
what the nature of God is becomes inscrutable.
Since "being," on Tillich's own account, makes no
determination about the kind of thing a particular
conception is, at best it tells us merely that the
notion of "God" can be conceived—though nothing
at all about what that conception is.

Now it is worthwhile to observe that Tillich
himself admits that "being," as an abstraction, is
"the emptiest of all concepts."[19] For as the basic
transcendentale, "being" precisely transcends all
genera; it transcends all predicates which determine something's particular nature. Tillich believes it is a necessary concept because it is that
without which the thought of any particular thing
could not take place. On the other hand, if being-
itself becomes the presupposition of any conceptual
act simply because it is, by definition, the property everything we conceive must have, that necessity
appears quite trivial.

[3]   What are we to make of this? I have pointed
out that when Tillich denies God is a particular
being, it is because he believes that "X is a (particular) being" entails that "X is a finite being"
(subject to the categories of substance, spatiality,
etc.) And it is just those categories which Tillich,
along with classical theology, denies are applicable
to God. The problem, however, is that in his desire

---

[19]ST II, p. 11.

to avoid identifying God with a particular being, in the sense just described, Tillich ultimately ends up identifying God with a property commonly predicable of all being. Now certainly when classical theologians denied that God is finite, they were not also denying that God is a singular individual. Indeed, the "perfections" of God point out in what way God must be a unique individual.

In Tillich's theology, however, the questions of God's finitude and God's singularity have become muddled. That is, when Tillich denies God is a being what he is intending to deny is only that God is finite—i.e., that God can be thought of as what is called a being "among others" or a being "beside others."[20] The confusion arises because Tillich conflates these. But denying that God is a being "among others" and denying that God is "a" being *simpliciter* are two distinct things. From the latter, but not the former, it follows that God is not a singular individual. From the former (God is not a being among others) it follows that God is not a finite being. But I do not think this follows from the denial that God is a being *simpliciter* because I am not sure it is really clear what follows from that, other than Tillich's idea that God, as being-itself, could be a property. However, that idea, as I will suggest, is incorrigible. As far as I can see, from the denial that God is a being *simpliciter* it might just as easily follow that

---

[20]ST I, pp. 172, 235; ST II, p. 23.

there is no God, in which case Tillich's concept
of being-itself has been wasted.

In any event, from the denial that God is a
finite being it need not follow that there is no
sense at all in which God could be thought of as a
singular individual. I think Tillich simply has
not seen this because he links the denial of God's
finitude to the claim that "God is being-itself."
As "being-itself," however, God is identified with
an obscure, logically non-determining transcendental attribute, shared by everything of which some
concept can be formed.

But that is incoherent. God cannot sensibly
be a property commonly possessed by everything.
What could it mean to say the God whom we worship
is an attribute of everything? How could the God
whom Tillich himself speaks of as the single creator of the world be an attribute of the world which
he creates? In short, if God is "the power of
being [which] must transcend every being that participates in it,"[21] then what sense does it make to
say that God is also identical with a property in-
herently possessed by every being? The answer
seems to be that it is not clear how it could make
any sense at all.

[4]   Finally, since this transcendental attribute,
common to every entity, cannot constitute the particular nature of any subject, then it cannot tell
us anything about the nature of God. It cannot,

---

[21]ST I, p. 231.

in other words, be the answer to the "question of
God" Tillich's analysis is supposed to lead us to.
For an analysis which leads to that which is predicable of anything and everything could not (logically could not) permit us to know what God is, if
God is that which must transcend anything and everything.

Yet "God is being-itself" is the only statement Tillich allows to literally inform us about
God's nature, so obviously there is some way Tillich thinks the predicate "being-itself" specifies
something. It is just that, however, which Tillich
not only fails to do but logically prohibits himself from doing. Thus, while Tillich both makes
and affirms many statements about God's nature in
the traditional language of the Church, unfortunately this does little to clarify what telling us that
God is "being-itself" tells us.

If the only answer to "the question of God"
is an answer which cannot be informative of anything about which the question asks, then the question must, as well as the answer, be regarded as
unintelligible. Further, since this universal but
non-determining predicate is what Tillich means
when he identifies God as "being-itself," then
Tillich's statement "God is being-itself" turns out
to be an incomplete expression. For if "God" refers in no sense to a singular existing individual,
then "God" cannot be a subject of which some predicate—even this most uninformative one—is true.
That is, "God is being-itself" means nothing more

than "Something or other is..." But that is an
incomplete expression. For the dots are meant to
hold a place for some further specifying predicate.
But since it is just that which Tillich does not
permit, the particular subject can never be identified.

When Tillich himself must finally say that
"being-itself" is the being which "means 'not being
anything special'"[22] because "it means being everything,"[23] one has the distinct impression that at
least Tillich's explanation of being-itself is incomplete. One wants to say: then being-itself can
be just anything at all.

                              ii

If we were to simply leave matters here, not
only would this view of God itself be unintelligible,
but it would also—as it turns out—be inconsistent
with certain other important features of Tillich's
theology which clearly indicate that there must be
a residual sense in which Tillich does allow that
God is a singular existing individual, despite his
claim that God is not a being. In defense of this
I will offer one preliminary remark and three specific arguments.

[1]   There are some indications Tillich was not
entirely satisfied with his account of "being-itself," and that he believed there needed to be a

---

[22]ST I, p. 188.

[23]Ibid.

way it could be understood as not the emptiest but
"the most meaningful of all concepts."[24] Tillich
describes this as the experience of a "power of
being which resists nonbeing."[25] Now insofar as
being-itself could be understood as a power—not in
the sense of a property intrinsic to all entities,
but in the sense of that which actually gives to
all things their power to be—then "being" would
strictly refer to the divine power which alone has
the "power to conquer nonbeing."

It should be made clear that Tillich in no
way consistently marks some special sense of "being"
applicable only to God. In fact, his own account
requires that the term be used univocally of God
and finite beings alike. So consistency is not one
of Tillich's virtues. Nevertheless, there are times
when Tillich hints at a distinction between two
kinds of beings: (a) the "being" possessed by finite
things—a being by "participation," and (b) pure
being or being-itself (the being of God).[26]

In sense (a) being is apparently "limited by"
or "mixed with" nonbeing. It is the being every finite thing has by participating in being-itself, but
which, nevertheless, is not "pure." In sense (b)
being is that power by which God is said to be "'by
himself'"; by which God "possesses 'aseity.'"[27]

---

[24] ST II, p. 11.

[25] *Ibid.*

[26] ST I, p. 189,   Cf. also ST I, p. 235.

[27] ST I, p. 236.

For "being-itself does not participate in non-being."[28]

Thus when Tillich makes the claim that "God is being-itself" he may not simply be meaning that God is the being predicable of everything, but that God is the inexhaustible source of the being which everything has. This is the claim, for example, that Aquinas had made when he said "God exists in everything by power inasmuch as everything is subject to his power."[29] That is, it is only in virtue of being subject to God's power that anything can have its own "power to conquer nonbeing." Thus, the power of being which everything "shares," may not, finally, be a power we possess; rather, it is something we have only by participating in being-itself, in which case we must have it derivatively. But then "being" is primarily predicable only of God, who is that from which all being derives.

Now while suggesting that it is possible to interpret Tillich as employing equivocal senses of "being," I think it is by no means necessary to interpret Tillich this way. For there are just as many reasons to regard him as having only one sense of "being" which must be applied univocally to everything, not the least of which is the fact that Tillich calls "being" a power inherent in everything.

---

[28] *Ibid.*

[29] Thomas Aquinas, *Summa Theologiae* Ia. Q. 8, art. 3, reply.

What these remarks do indicate, however, is
that Tillich seems willing to assign God the singularity required in order to make God understand-
able as the single source ultimately responsible
for a property of "being" which is also (however
paradoxically) in some sense intrinsic to everything.

[2]   It is quire clear that Tillich makes many
dogmatic claims about God, more or less in the
language of the "traditional theism" he sometimes
seems so bent on rejecting. For example:

> God transcends...the world.
> God participates in everything that is;
> he has community with it.
> God is spirit.
> God is infinite.
> God is creative.
> God *has* created the world, he *is* creative
> in the present moment, and he *will* cre-
> atively fulfill his *telos*.
> God creates man.[30]

Tillich also finds it intelligible to speak of God
as "living" or refer to God as "Lord" or "Father."
Thus, despite the fact that Tillich denies God can
be a being, in many dogmatic assertions Tillich
himself treats God as a singular individual. For
in all of these statements, the subject term "God"
is used as a logically proper name. That is, it
names some particular individual about whom something is being asserted.

What brings out the sense in which "God" is
used as a logically proper name most clearly are

---

[30]Respectively, ST I, p. 237, 245, 249, 252,
253, 256.

occasions when Tillich uses the term "God" in direct address: "Almighty God! We raise our hearts
to thee in praise and thanks.... We thank thee that
we have being.... We are gratefully aware of thy
presence...."[31] Here, the singular personal pronoun is used as a substitute for "God." But this
is only possible if God is the individual to which
"thee" can sensibly refer.

Now Tillich qualifies the traditional utterances he makes about God by calling them "symbolic."
But how is this relevant? If the issue were whether God should literally be called a person, the
qualification would be relevant since Tillich clearly resists the anthropomorphism that God is no more
than "a heavenly, completely perfect person who re-
sides above the world and mankind."[32] The issue
here, however, is quite distinct—for it is the
more fundamental question of whether Tillich treats
God as a singular individual in any sense. And
calling dogmatic statements about God "symbolic"
simply does not alter that question. For Tillich
has nowhere shown how it is possible to make any
number of true symbolic statements in which the
term "God" is used as the name of a singular individual, even though the assumption that God is a
singular being is false.

The fact is that most of Tillich's "symbolic"
statements about God would clearly be unintelligible

[31]Paul Tillich, "In Everything Give Thanks,"
The Eternal Now (London: SCM Press, 1963), p. 157.

[32]ST I, p. 245.

unless it could be assumed that they were about
some individual. In many symbolic statements, for
example, a metaphor, which could only be used of a
singular being, is used as a substitute for the
term "God": "From the point of view of the creator,
the purpose of creation is the exercise of his creativity..."[33] Now if Tillich did not mean to allow
that God is an individual in any sense, it would
make no sense to even qualify the statement as
"symbolic": for there would be nothing for which
the term "creator" could function as a symbol.
That is, there would be nothing to which the "symbolic" term could refer about which the assertion
of its creativity is being made. Tillich's dogmatic claims about God thus commit him to the view
that God is a singular individual.[34]

[3]   We have seen that what entails that God is
not a being is the identification of God with
"being-itself." At the same time, however, Tillich
is not at all uncomfortable using the term "being-
itself" as an irreducible singular subject. Tillich
has no objection to treating "being-itself" as if
it named some individual when he proclaims "there
is of course that being which is beyond essence and

---

[33]ST I, p. 263.

[34]Tillich explicitly states that a symbol for
an individual can be understood as a symbol for God
when he says that in "the image of a highest being...
we have a symbol for that which is not symbolic in
the idea of God——namely, 'Being-itself.'" "The Nature of Religious Language," *Theology of Culture*,
p. 61.

existence, which...we call God——or, if you prefer,
'being-itself,'"[35] or when he informs us that being-
itself has "qualities"[36] and "manifestations."[37]
In short, Tillich is not uncomfortable using "being-
itself as an irreducible abstract proper name when
he makes it the singular subject of statements in
which something is predicated about whatever is de-
noted by "being-itself."

Consider the following remarks:

> Being-itself is beyond finitude and infinity;
>   otherwise it would be conditioned by some-
>   thing other than itself....
> Being-itself manifests itself to finite being
>   in the infinite drive of the finite beyond
>   itself.[38]

In each of these statements Tillich gives himself
the syntactical warrant for talking about being-
itself as if it existed as a singular individual,
in spite of the fact that he has denied it could
be.

Now it should be pointed out that the use of
an abstract singular expression as the subject of
a sentence does not necessarily imply that it is
being used as a logically proper name. For example,
when one says "Wisdom is a feature of some men," it

---

[35]Brown, ed., *Ultimate Concern*, p. 45.

[36]ST I, p. 44.

[37]ST I, p. 207.

[38]Respectively, ST I, p. 237, 191.

can be argued that "wisdom" is not the name of any
single entity over against the various instances
in which it is true of something on the grounds
that it is possible to replace this "name" (nominalization) by the concrete predicate from which
it is derived. Proof of this is the fact that the
sentence can equally read as: "Some men are wise."
But a sentence in which this is not possible—a
sentence in which such a nominalization of a predicate is used as an irreducible abstract proper
name—commits one to the view that there is some
single entity which it names beyond the instances
in which it can be predicated of something.[39]

What I am suggesting, then, is that in statements such as the ones cited, "being-itself" is
used as an irreducible proper name. In the statement "Being-itself infinitely transcends every finite being," for example, there does not seem to be
any obvious way to read out "being-itself" as the
singular subject of a transitive verb by replacing
it with a predicate that is used of some other subject. Furthermore, attaching the reflexive pronoun
"-itself" gramatically indicates that "being-itself"
is treated as a singular individual. Thus, his own
usage commits Tillich to a position in which "being-
itself" must be regarded as the "name" of some
single individual.

[4]   The preceding two points have indicated that
Tillich often treats God as an individual. My last

---

[39]Cf. Peter Geach, "Form and Existence," *God
and the Soul* (New York: Schocken Books, 1969), pp. 46-7.

point urges that his own analysis of God in terms
of the polar concepts of "individuality" and "participation" logically binds him to do so.

First, a word about what a "polar" concept is
and then how Tillich uses them. In general, a
"polar" concept is simply a concept which would not
be intelligible without implying a relation to an
opposite with which it is contrasted. For example,
when we use the predicate "...is alive" of something,
this makes sense because we are able to contrast
that thing with other things to which it is possible
to apply the predicate "...is dead." The concept
of "being alive," in other words, would not be
meaningful without the possibility of elsewhere employing its polar opposite.

Tillich's use of the concepts of "individuality" and "participation" is similar in the sense
that they contrast with one another. What is different is that they are not mutually exclusive as
"dead" and "alive" are. That is, it would not, according to Tillich, be possible to speak something
as an individual without also implying that it can
be an individual only because of its participation
with other beings.[40]

Now both of these concepts must be asserted
of God equally—the grammatical fact Tillich sometimes characterizes as an "inescapable inner ten-
sion" within the idea of God. Thus, while we have
seen Tillich appear to deny that God is a being,

---

[40]ST I, p. 174 ff and 244 ff.

his objection, in fact, is to representing God as
only (exclusively) an individual. This is the mistake of "ordinary theism." For that view has emphasized only one side of the polarity of individuality and participation: it has represented God
solely as an absolute individual. However, Tillich
denies it is meaningful to do this. Tillich's
point is that the only sense in which it is meaningful to speak of God as the absolute individual
is that in which it is equally meaningful to speak
of God as the "absolute participant."[41] "The one
term cannot be applied without the other."[42]

What Tillich is anxious about is that in emphasizing God as an absolute individual, we have
forgotten that "God is the principle of participation as well as the principle of individualization.
The divine life participates in every life as its
ground and aim. God participates in everything
that is; he has community with it; he shares in its
destiny."[43] Tillich thinks it is wrong to regard
God only as an individual because he identifies absolute individualization as a form of metaphysical
"solitude."[44] From the standpoint of God's creativity, however—i.e., God's creation of the world and
his participation in it—the notion of a God who

---

[41] ST I, p. 244. Cf. also Stuart Brown, *Do
Religious Claims Make Sense?* (New York: The Macmillan Company, 1969), p. 196.

[42] ST I, p. 244.

[43] ST I, p. 245.

[44] Cf. ST II, p. 65.

remains in absolute solitude is inconceivable.

But if it is impossible to speak of God as
an individual being without implying that God is
also the being which participates in everything,
then it should be equally clear that it is impossible to speak of God as the "absolute participant"
without, at the same time, implying that God is
also an individual. For these "polar" concepts
work just that way: viz., one cannot be meaningfully used without the other.

We can conclude, then, that in Tillich's view,
God or "being-itself," at least in a residual sense
is a singular individual. This is called a "residual" sense only because Tillich often seems preoc-
cupied with showing what he believes goes wrong
when the pole of "individuality" in the concept of
God is emphasized to exclude any ground for God's
"participation" in the world. Nevertheless, it is
Tillich himself who makes "individuality" logically
part of his concept of God. That is, being-itself
necessarily has this "double characteristic."[45]

Individuality, then, must be seen not merely
as the polar opposite of participation but also as
its presupposition: for "the more individualized a
being is, the more it is able to participate."[46]
Thus, while Tillich is concerned that God's "participation" in the world is a feature of the concept
of God theology has neglected, his own analysis of

---

[45]ST I, p. 237.

[46]ST II, p. 65.

"participation" as a polar concept entails God's
individuality as its logically necessary counter-
part. From Tillich's denial that God is a being,
then, it cannot follow that God is in no sense at
all a singular individual.

CHAPTER THREE

A FORM OF ONTOLOGICAL ARGUMENT

Tillich is widely held to be among those Protestant theologians who proclaim considerable scepticism about the arguments for the existence of God. This particular form of scepticism is not an attack on any individual argument or set of arguments, but rather is a wholesale rejection of the possibility of there being any "argument" for the existence of God at all.

The best evidence for attributing this view to Tillich derives from his own testimony. According to Tillich, "there can be little doubt that the arguments are a failure insofar as they claim to be arguments."[1] The primary reason cited for this "failure" is the suggestion that "the method of arguing to a conclusion"[2] is "inadequate for the idea of God";[3] indeed, it "contradicts the idea of God."[4]

More precisely, Tillich seems to hold that God's existence cannot be made a matter of inference from any given data about the world because

---

[1] ST I, p. 204.

[2] *Ibid.*

[3] *Ibid.*

[4] ST I, p. 205.

that method of argument is inconsistent with a
proper understanding of the concept of God:

> Every argument derives conclusions from
> something that is sought. In arguments
> for the existence of God the world is
> given and God is sought. Some character-
> istics of the world make the conclusion
> "God" necessary. God is derived from the
> world.[5]

In contrast, Tillich claims the belief that God can
be derived from the world opposes the idea of a
transcendent God: "if we derive God from the world,
he cannot be that which transcends the world infinitely."[6] The concept of a transcendent God and
arguments which depend on "characteristics of the
world" are, therefore, contradictory.

Since Tillich does not offer any defense of
this view there is little to say about it as it
stands. However, it is curious that Tillich makes
these remarks at the beginning of his analysis "rejecting" the ontological argument since the criticism, of course, is relevant to the cosmological
argument. In fact, it is precisely the appeal of
the ontological argument that God's existence is
not made a matter of inference from any given data—
from some objective feature of the world—but rather
is discovered to be the presupposition of our ability to conceive of God at all.

It turns out that Tillich displays a rather

---

[5] ST I, p. 205.

[6] *Ibid.*

peculiar attitude toward the ontological argument.
First, he does not regard it as really an "argument." Second, his explanation of why the ontological argument is "no argument at all"[7] is ambiguous:

> The question of God is possible because
> an awareness of God is present in the
> question of God. This awareness precedes
> the question. It is not the result of the
> argument but its presupposition.[8]

Is Tillich offering us a reason to "reject" the
ontological argument or is he making some form of
it necessary?

I think it is correct to interpret these remarks as suggesting, in part, that it is in some
way intrinsic to the concept of God that God is
identical with that of which it is impossible "not
to be aware." That is, in even raising "the question of God" we somehow come to discover that we
are already aware of God. But from this, according
to Tillich, it also follows that we cannot meaningfully ask the question of whether God exists.

> ...there is no place to which man can
> withdraw from the divine thou, because it
> includes the ego and is nearer to the ego
> than the ego to itself. Ultimately, it is
> an insult to the divine holiness to talk
> about God as we do of objects whose exist-
> ence or nonexistence can be discussed.[9]

---

[7] ST I, p. 206.

[8] *Ibid.*

[9] ST I, p. 271. Cf. also Tillich, "Escape From God," in *The Shaking of the Foundations*
p. 47.

Tillich's indictment of the question of the existence of God as "meaningless" is made with considerable frequency:

> ...the question of the existence of God
> can neither be asked nor answered.   If
> it is asked...the answer—whether negative
> or affirmative—implicitly denies the na-
> ture of God.[10]

> ...the discussions about the existence or
> nonexistence of God [are] meaningless.[11]

From the above it is clear that what Tillich rather
loosely calls "the question of God" needs to be
distinguished from a further question he considers:
viz., "the question of God's existence." The former question is one that it is possible to meaningfully ask; the latter is not.

"The question of God" is a possible question
because the concept of "God" is intelligible.   In
asking it, presumably we are asking about what "God"
is.   "The question of God's existence," however, is
not a possible question. But it is not so as a result of a certain feature Tillich attaches to the
former question: viz., that an awareness of God is
present in "the question of God" and this awareness
is a presupposition of our asking it. The former
question, then, establishes the basis for the im-
possibility of the latter.

What seems, in effect, to be happening is that
Tillich regards the question of God's existence as
"meaningless" only because he begs the question. If

---

[10]ST I, p. 237.

[11]Tillich, *Dynamics of Faith*, p. 46. See also
"The Philosophy of Religion,", p. 71: "It is meaningless to ask...whether the Unconditioned 'exists'..."

it is possible, as Tillich seems to think it is, to speak of an "awareness" of God which always precedes any question of his existence, then the question of whether God exists is "meaningless" precisely because Tillich has assumed there is necessarily only one possible answer to it even before it is asked.

Further, it is important to note that this awareness of God in "the question of God" must have the force of logical (not just psychological) necessity[12] in order for Tillich to be able to call "the question of God's existence" meaningless. One might, for example, think Tillich is simply saying that God's presence is so powerful in our awareness that to question his existence is psychologically unimaginable. This would be wrong because it would miss just that sense in which Tillich claims the question of God's existence to be meaningless: viz., that any answer to the question—yes or no— is meaningless. In short, Tillich argues the question is nonsense.

Of course, the psychological fact of any awareness of God is contingent upon my having it. Nor does this bear on the linguistic fact that one can still sensibly ask the general question: But is there, after all, a God?[13] To call that question

---

[12]In other words, the awareness must be logically prior to the question.

[13]Moreover, I can sensibly ask this question of myself even given "my awareness" of God, because I can question whether my awareness is veridical.

meaningless presupposes that to simply state the
question is to commit some logical absurdity. Thus,
Tillich is guilty of begging the question just because he says there can be no answer either way
(the question is nonsense, improper), yet he assumes there is one (moreover, only one).

Far from rejecting all forms of argument for
God's existence, then, Tillich himself seems committed to some version of one. It runs, roughly,
as follows: If one properly understands the concept "God" to mean "that of which it is impossible
not to be aware" (God "includes the ego; an awareness of God is the "presupposition" of the question
of God) then it is senseless to raise the question
of God's existence. It is senseless to question
the existence of that of whose presence one logically cannot be unaware.

The reason for thinking Tillich intends this
is made stronger by his insistence that we are "immediately" aware[14] of God's presence in the question of God. According to Tillich, "man is immediately aware of something unconditional";[15] "...the
ontological awareness [of the Unconditioned] is immediate, and not mediated by inferential processes.
It is present, whenever conscious attention is fo-
cussed on it, in terms of an unconditional certain-

---

[14]Tillich, "The Two Types of Philosophy
of Religion," p. 22.

[15]Ibid.

ty."[16]   Indeed, "the immediate awareness of the
Unconditioned has not the character of faith but of
self-evidence."[17]

Tillich apparently holds, then, that there is
an awareness we must have of God which renders his
existence both self-evident and indubitable:

> It is meaningless to ask...whether the
> Unconditional "exists,".... For the
> question whether the Unconditional exists
> presupposes already...that which exists
> unconditionally. The certainty of the
> Unconditional is the grounding certainty
> from which all doubt can proceed, but it
> can never itself be the object of doubt.
> Therefore, the object of religion is not
> only real, but is also the presupposition
> of every affirmation of reality.[18]

Thus, Tillich has "built into" his concept of God a
sense of necessity that ranges over our awareness
of God, as a result of which he regards it as
senseless to raise the question of his existence.

This form of argument is also displayed in
Tillich's identification of God with "being-itself."
Here, instead of saying with the ontological argument that God necessarily exists, Tillich implies
that God's reality is a necessity of thought when
anything is said to exist. Being-itself, according
to Tillich, is that "which is always thought implicitly and sometimes explicitly, if something is

[16] *Ibid.*, p. 23.

[17] *Ibid.*, p. 27.

[18] Tillich, "The Philosophy of Religion," p. 71.

said to be."[19]   However, being-itself is not simply an object of thought; it is also something
which itself exists. That is, being-itself is the
Unconditional which itself "exists unconditionally...[and] can never itself be the object of doubt."
Moreover, that which is the presupposition of all
thought——"the presupposition of every affirmation
of reality"——must itself exist because our immediate awareness of it in thought has given its existence the character of "self-evidence."

ii

Thus far I have intended only to give a rough
picture of how Tillich's analysis of the concept of
God bears some relation to the ontological argument. I think the evidence that there is a connection is sufficiently convincing to warrant further
examination of the several remarks Tillich has to
make about Anselm and the argument itself.

To begin with, Tillich indicates that he accepts as valid what he calls the "Anselmian statement."

> ...the Anselmian statement that God is a
> necessary thought and that therefore this
> idea must have objective as well as sub-
> jective reality is valid insofar as think-
> ing, by its very nature, implies an un-
> conditional element which transcends sub-
> jectivity and objectivity...[20]

---

[19]ST I, p. 163.

[20]ST I, p. 207.

This is not the clearest "statement" nor is it the clearest restatement of Anselm. Nevertheless, it is clear enough to see that at least Tillich agrees with some position whose conclusion is this: (1) the concept of God is subjectively intelligible; (2) it has an instance, in some sense, in objective reality.

Let us bracket for the moment the business about precisely how "thinking implies an unconditional element" since I will return to that shortly. (It is, in any case, a consideration that does not substantially alter the possibility of seeing Tillich as making the above claims.) What I want to consider first is the rather surprising fact that Tillich seems to want to deny that the ontological "statement" demonstrates the existence of God: "the statement is not valid if this unconditional element is understood as a highest being called God."[21] Nor can "the experience of an unconditional element in a man's encounter with reality [be] used for the establishment of an unconditional being (a contradiction in terms) within reality."[22]

It is hard to know what to make of this. In the first place Tillich cannot be worrying about the validity of Anselm's deduction, since he doesn't even state it. Consequently his "rejection" of the argument—for whatever reason—cannot be directed at the logical form of the argument itself. What is

---

[21] *Ibid.*

[22] *Ibid.*

perplexing is that Tillich accepts the conclusion
of the argument as valid on the one hand, yet then
appears to deny that the conclusion has anything
to do with the existence of God.

The issue forced out seems to be that of
equivocation. The equivocation here is not, as it
might first appear, between the "objective reality"
and the "existence" of God, but between two different senses of the term "God" Tillich inadvertently
uses.[23] To bring this out more clearly consider
what it is that Tillich is denying. Tillich denies that the ontological "statement" can establish
the existence of "a highest being" or "an unconditional being" within reality. The ambiguity of
these remarks lies in the fact that a highest being
or an unconditional being "within reality" is precisely what Tillich could not mean by "God." Why?
Simply, because to be "a" (singular) being is to
be within reality, where "within" has the force of
"exists as a conditioned part of." More exactly,
to be "within reality," on Tillich's account, is
identical with membership in the class of "the totality of beings."[24] But God, properly understood
as the ground of being, "cannot be found within the
totality of beings."[25] The reason is that membership in this class entails being "subject to the

---

[23]However, sometimes Tillich equivocates on
the term "exists" as well, as has often been pointed
out.

[24]ST I, p. 205.

[25]*Ibid.*

categories of finitude."[26]

Now, clearly something could not be both "subject to the categories of finitude"—i.e., a spatio-temporal object, an object "conditioned by space and time"—and also identical with God who is unconditioned. However, it is important to note that the whole matter arises as a result of the rather arbitrary entailment relation Tillich sees between membership in the class of "the totality of beings within reality" and the notion of finitude. Traditionally, of course, it has been regarded as possible to say that God is a member of the class of the total number of beings within reality, only a unique member of that class. For Tillich, however, that is quite impossible: for, by definition, a being "within the totality of beings" is a finite being—even if it is the highest being in that class. And God, of course, cannot be a finite being.[27] On the other hand, Tillich's "rejection" of the ontological argument now seems quite misplaced. For Tillich does not deny that the argument establishes the existence of God as Tillich thinks "God" must be understood (viz., as being-itself), but only that it does not establish the existence of an unconditional being "within the totality of beings." Yet since that is precisely what Tillich does not

---

[26]ST I, p. 235.

[27]Consequently, Tillich calls "an unconditioned being" a "contradiction in terms" because to be "a" being is to be within reality and therefore to be conditioned.

mean by "God," who, as Tillich also puts it, is
not a being "among others,"[28] it remains entirely
open that he is committed to such an argument insofar as it establishes what Tillich thinks must
be God.

The question, then, is this. Is Tillich committed, if not to a formal argument, to some ontological "principle" which establishes the existence of God when "God" is understood as being-itself? It is my intuition that Tillich is. Since
Tillich himself has no explicit argument to offer,
it is difficult to identify the moves involved.
Nevertheless, whatever form of argument it is, it
is associated with Tillich's view of the relation
between God as being-itself and the nature of
"thinking," and what must be presupposed in order
for it to be possible for there to be thought at
all.

According to Tillich, there is a "principle"[29]
that lies within the ontological "statement" which
awakens us to the discovery that God is being-itself. Furthermore, since being-itself is the presupposition of all thought, it is consequently
the presupposition of any possible conception of
God.

Now Tillich says he wants to accept the
"principle" of the ontological argument only, not

---

[28] ST I, p. 172.

[29] Tillich, "The Two Types of Philosophy of
Religion," p. 22.

the conclusion (viz., that God exists). But I see
no reason to believe that Tillich is not committed
to the conclusion as well. For being-itself, as we
have seen, must have not only subjective but also
objective reality. Thus, since being-itself is
identical with God, the objective reality of God
must be the presupposition not only for any possible concept of God but for the possibility of any
thought at all.

Because being-itself is the presupposition of
all thought, it is, according to Tillich, "a necessary thought."[30] It is that behind which thought
"cannot go," that on which thought is "based."[31]
It is that which must be thought whenever something
is said to be. Being-itself is the unconditional
element in our encounter with reality which transcends subjectivity and objectivity.[32] It is something of which we have an immediate awareness, and
which transcends the distinction, in any analysis of
thought, between the thinking subject and that which
thought is about.

While not everything Tillich says here is entirely clear, I think it is clear that, according to
Tillich, Anselm's argument views God as a "necessity
of thought" in this way. That is, Tillich understands Anselm's "statement" to be the statement "that
God is a necessary thought...an unconditional element

---

[30] *Ibid.*, p. 15.

[31] ST I, p. 163.

[32] Cf. ST I, p. 207.

in man's encounter with reality" which is the basis
of all thought. Thus, it seems reasonable to assume that Tillich thinks Anselm has in mind what he
has in mind by being-itself.

Furthermore, Tillich thinks Anselm is right
in claiming this idea has objective reality, because
Tillich believes that thought itself presupposes the
reality of being-itself. That is, when God is understood as being-itself—a necessity of thought—
then Anselm is right when he argues "that therefore
this idea must have objective as well as subjective
reality." Why does Tillich think Anselm is right?
Anselm is right because he has recognized that
thinking itself—the very nature of thought—presupposes the existence of being-itself. Consequently, since Tillich accepts from Anselm that being-
itself has objective reality, it would seem that
Tillich has accepted this as an argument that being-
itself must be.

There are, one can say, two steps to Tillich's
interpretation of Anselm's argument. For Tillich,
it is part of the concept of "thinking" that (1) we
necessarily think of being-itself if we are to think
of anything at all (being-itself has subjective reality), and (2) being-itself must be (being-itself
has objective reality).

iii

I suggest we now examine more carefully what
Tillich means when he identifies being-itself as
the "objective presupposition of all thought."
Tillich says that being-itself "remains the content, the mystery, and the eternal *aporia* of
thinking."[33] It is "the basis of the being of all
things whereby 'being' is taken absolutely, trans-
cendentally as the expression of the secret into
which thinking cannot penetrate, because as something existing it itself is based on it."[34]

Sometimes, however, Tillich tries to make
this "secret into which thinking cannot penetrate"
explicit. In Tillich's view, thinking requires "a
point of identity [between subject and object]
which makes the idea of truth possible."[35] This
point of identity, present in every true judgment,
is being-itself. The unconditional element which
"transcends" subjectivity and objectivity is "the
Absolute in which the difference between knowing
and known is not actual."[36] Furthermore, "this

---

[33]ST II, p. 11.

[34]Paul Tillich, *The Interpretation of History*
(trans. by N. A. Rasetzki and Elsa L. Talmey; New
York: Charles Scribner's Sons, 1936), p. 83, quoted
in Adams, *Paul Tillich's Philosophy of Culture,
Science, and Religion,* p. 45.

[35]ST I, p. 207.

[36]Tillich, "The Two Types of Philosophy of
Religion," p. 15.

Absolute as the principle of Being has absolute
certainty. It is a necessary thought because it is
the presupposition of all thought."[37]

What, first of all, does Tillich mean by the
"point of identity" between subject and object
which makes truth possible? What does he mean by
the idea that being-itself, as that which subject
and object share in common, "transcends" their
separation?

Tillich's analysis of thinking entails that
the distinction between subject and object be regarded as an ontological separation. On Tillich's
account, any intelligible experience of an object
consists not simply in having a certain relation to
some object external to the thought of it, but entails, in some manner, a uniting of subject and object.[38] "Knowing" is said to be a "union" in which
"the knower participates in the known."[39]

Because the separation between the thinking
subject and any object is viewed as a real separation, to think that some x is *F* must involve, according to Tillich, a real participation in the form
(what Tillich also refers to as an object's "true
being")[40] which constitutes the essence of that x.
When one thinks of some *F*-ness, what exists in the
subject is not just a relation to the *F*-ness of that

---

[37] *Ibid.*

[38] Cf. ST I, p. 94.

[39] ST I, p. 177.

[40] ST I, p. 101.

object; rather, there is a union such that what exists in the subject, in some sense, is that *F*-ness.

Tillich is not saying that when I have a thought of something, say, of a stone, I somehow become identical with the stone, or that it is the stone itself which is in my mind. Rather, my thought is an occurrence of an "essential structure" which is in some sense the same or identical with another individual occurrence in that stone: "The particular object is strange [ontologically separate] as such, but it contains essential structures with which the cognitive subject is essentially united and which it can remember when looking at things."[41]

Tillich, however, never fully explains in what sense my thinking that x is *F* is the "same" form as occurs in x. To avoid the suggestion that it is the stone which is in my head, Tillich seems to regard the distinction between a thing's "essence" and its "being" as a real distinction. What my thought is "united" with is the essence of the stone, not its "own" being. But the essence of that stone is not "in my head" either, and Tillich's account not only remains largely unclear, but, further, his talk of a union between myself and the stone doesn't do much to alleviate the idea that I—in my head—somehow become that stone.

---

[41]ST I, pp. 94-95.

[42]Brown, ed., *Ultimate Concern*, p. 45, Cf. also ST II, p. 21.

Finally, there is a distinct sense in which to know that some x "is a stone" I must participate in (i.e., share) its "own" being. For Tillich argues that "the essences of things...have being, too."[42] At this point the ontological distinction between essence and being simply dissolves. For if the essence of a stone is not only that which is common to all stones, but also the "being" individuated in each particular stone, then my participation in the essence of that stone is identical with participation in its "own" being.

In any case, insofar as there is a sense of "being" which is common to both me and the stone in each thought of a stone, there is a being we both share. This common sense of "being"—that by which there is a union between the being of the knower and the being of the known—is the "unconditional element which transcends subjectivity and objectivity," the "Absolute" Tillich refers to as being-itself. This is the "point of identity" which makes truth possible. It is "actually present"[43] in both the subject and the object, and what makes it possible to speak of the form in my mind and the form of that stone as the same form. Since it is present in both the subject and the object, it "transcends" that ontological separation, and as such becomes that which the thought of anything presupposes.

By laying emphasis on the idea that the reality of being-itself is a necessary presupposition

[43]Cf. ST I, p. 192.

for all thought, Tillich has in effect replaced the
concept of a "necessary being" with the notion of
that being which is necessary for thinking. Tillich's remark that thought itself is "something
existing," and must, therefore, be based on being[44]
indicates why Tillich feels he must accept Anselm's
statement that being-itself has objective reality.
Since thinking, in Tillich's view, is never simply
a subjective phenomenon, it always involves a real
participation of the knower in the being of that
which is known. Thinking, therefore, always has
objective reality. Thus, if God is being-itself,
and if thinking presupposes the objective reality
of being-itself, one can see why Tillich's reflection on the presuppositions of thought leads him to
the conclusion that in "thinking" we must be immediately aware of the presence of God.

This somewhat involuted argument for the reality of God can be found in Tillich's earliest
works. The ontological reality of God is described
as a matter of immediate awareness to the self—an
awareness upon which the possibility of any self-
awareness, indeed of any knowledge at all, must be
based:

> ...the self grasps within itself the Uncondi-
> tional as the basis of its own self-certainty...
> the Unconditional is neither object nor sub-
> ject, but rather the presupposition for every
> possible antithesis of subject and object...
> the Unconditional is certainly the supporting
> ground of every theoretical judgment...there

---

[44]Tillich, *The Interpretation of History*, p.
83, quoted in Adams, *op. cit.*, p. 45.

> can be absolutely no certainty in which
> the certainty of God is not implicite
> present.[45]

Moreover, the certainty of God's reality is self-evident: "the certainty of the Unconditional is unconditional."[46]

Despite Tillich's insistence that he can accept only the principle of the ontological argument but not its conclusion, then, he is clearly committed to its conclusion as well. Tillich wants to say the argument is not about the existence of God but about the nature of thought. Nevertheless, Tillich's analysis of the nature of thinking entails the objective reality of being-itself. Indeed, its existence cannot be subject to doubt, for it is "affirmed" in every statement which attempts to deny it.[47] But being-itself and God are identical. Hence, Tillich's analysis of thought entails the existence of God. It is not so much that Tillich fails to see this, but that he simply refuses to make the conclusion explicit.

iv

One must acknowledge that Tillich's interpretation of Anselm's argument is not itself an argu-

---

[45]Paul Tillich, "The Conquest of the Concept of Religion in the Philosophy of Religion," in *What Is Religion?*, pp. 139-40.

[46]*Ibid.*, p. 124.

[47]Tillich, "The Two Types of Philosophy of Religion," p. 13.

ment. It is, rather, a claim about an argument—
and a claim that is none too clear at that. Why,
for example, does Tillich seem to agree that being-
itself is "known in such a way that it cannot be
thought not to be,"[48] but also hold that the ontological argument is not really an argument for God?
By examining one further aspect of Tillich's grounds
for "rejecting" the argument, we can see why Tillich
holds such a view.

Tillich thinks there is a general line of
criticism of the argument which can be made[49] and
which is right: namely, that there cannot be "a
logical transition from the necessity of Being itself to a highest being, from a principle which is
beyond essence and existence to something that exists."[50] While it is not entirely clear just what
transition Tillich thinks cannot be made, it seems
reasonable enough to assume that the remark is meant
as a version of a certain line of criticism that
runs: one cannot argue from conceptual being to
being in reality. That is, from an investigation
of certain features intrinsic to a given concept one
cannot determine whether that concept has any instances. Now Tillich states that his "ontological
way is not a logical conclusion from the idea of the
Unconditioned to its existence...a procedure that,

---

[48]*Ibid.*, p. 15.

[49]And which has been made "from Gaunilo and
Thomas to Kant." *Ibid.*

[50]*Ibid.*

of course, is impossible."[51] The problem, however,
is that Tillich has no objection to talking of
"ideas" necessarily presupposed in thinking as themselves having being. We have already seen how
being-itself must be presupposed to have being when
Tillich accepts Anselm's argument that this "idea"
must have not only subjective but also objective
reality. However, there are other "less universal"[52] ontological concepts and categories,[53] con-
stituting the "structure" of being-itself, which
also have being. In fact, according to Tillich,
"everything which can be conceptualized must have
being."[54]

Tillich's use of "being" is indeed ubiquitous,
and appears to commit him to an extreme form of realism similar to that once held by Russell: "Being
is that which belongs to every conceivable term, to
every possible object of thought...being is a general attribute of everything, and to mention anything is to show that it is."[55]

---

[51]Tillich, "The Conquest of the Concept of
Religion in the Philosophy of Religion," p. 129.

[52]That is, less universal that being-itself,
but more universal than class concepts "designating
a realm of being." (ST I, p. 164).

[53]Namely, the concepts of individuality and
participation, dynamics and form, freedom and destiny, and the general categories of space, time,
casuality, and substance. (ST I, pp. 164-75).

[54]ST I, p. 179.

[55]Bertrand Russell, *The Principles of Mathematics* (2nd edition; New York: W. W. Norton and
Company, 1937), p. 449.

What does Tillich have in mind by the thesis
according to which everything that can be conceived
must have being? I suggest Tillich is attempting
to provide some sort of general principle upon
which the existence of God as being-itself must be
presupposed. For if the reality of God is the presupposition of any argument for his existence,
Tillich apparently feels he can avoid the problems
he believes are attached to any method of "arguing
through a conclusion" in which a logical move from
idea to existence is involved. That is, by getting
us to admit to the reality of certain concepts presupposed by thought, Tillich believes we will be
led to an awareness of an ultimate concept, being-
itself, whose existence is the necessary presupposition of our being able to entertain any concept
at all.

There are two kinds of concepts whose reality
Tillich is interested in having us acknowledge. In
ascending order of abstraction, they are: (1) the
concepts of essences which distinguish things into
"classes,"[56] or what Tillich sometimes calls non-
actualized possible beings,[57] and (2) the general
ontological concepts that are universally predicable,

---

[56]For example, the essence "treehood." (Cf.
ST II, p. 21).

[57]Cf. ST II, p. 20. See also Brown, ed.,
Ultimate Concern, p. 45, where Tillich refers to
the "potentialities of existence which we usually
call the essences of things...they have being, too;
they are the power of being, which may become
beings."

applicable to the members of every class.[58]

Beyond them lies the concept of that which
is most universal—being-itself. It is more universal than even those general ontological concepts
applicable to things of every class, because "being"
must be applied to every concept itself.[59] It is
in this sense that Tillich calls being "the basic
transcendentale, beyond the universal and the particular."[60] The notion of a concept of being which
is utterly universal, incidentally, also lies behind Tillich's rejection of nominalism's claim that
"universals...have no reality of their own."[61] For
Tillich denies that "Being as such...does not designate anything real"[62] in his claim that it must
have objective reality. But if being-itself designates something real, then all concepts—including
universals—must designate something real as well,
since something is a possible concept only by virtue
of its participation in being-itself, the presupposition of all thought. Getting us to admit the reality of these two classes of concepts less universal than being-itself thus "points to" the reality of
being-itself. For only by participating in being-
itself can they share the "being" Tillich claims

---

[58]For example, the general ontological concepts of individuality and participation.

[59]ST I, p. 179,

[60]ST II, p. 11.

[61]ST II, p. 10.

[62]ST II, p. 11.

must belong to every concept.

If Tillich's use of "being" as a universal
predicate is a paradigm of his ontology of thinking,
the question is how this usage results in a position from which Tillich thinks he can eliminate the
worry of an illegitimate transition from concept to
reality in his own version of Anselm's "statement."
Tillich's doctrine that "being" is a universal predicate has two relevant features. The first is
stated in Tillich's claim that "everything which
can be conceptualized must have being." This statement urges the general view that whatever we conceive, we must conceive to have being: i.e., we
can't conceive of anything without also attributing
being to it. Hence, "being" is made the necessary
property of every possible object of which we have
some concept.[63]

The second feature is implicit in the first,
but can be brought out in the following way. From
the general form of Tillich's doctrine there follows
a further claim: viz., that "all concepts" are themselves included as members of "everything which can
be conceptualized" and must, therefore, have being.[64]
Here, in other words, it is the concept itself that
becomes the object. Now while a "concept" is
clearly not some thing—it "cannot be thought of
something that is"[65]—neither, according to Tillich,

---

[63] Cf. ST II, p. 20.

[64] ST I, p. 179.

[65] *Ibid.*

"can it be thought of something that is not."[66]
It must, in some way, have being, since it can itself be conceptualized, or thought about. Further,
it must itself have form: for "there is no being
without form"[67] "Being," then, is a necessary
property not only of every existing object, but of
every conception itself.

The consequence of the doctrine that "being"
is a universal predicate is simply to identify the
being of the conception with the being of what is
conceived. With respect to "being," concepts and
objects share the same thing: i.e., there is an
identity between the formal reality of every concept we entertain and its objective reality, because concepts are said to participate in the same
being as do existing objects. Thus, there is no
ontological distinction between the fact that we
can entertain some concept and the objective reality of that concept.

It is, then, the very ubiquity of Tillich's
use of the term "being" that obviates the possibility of any "transition" from concept to reality.
Since "being" is that which has transcendental application, no question of any transition can even
arise. "Being" must be involved in every conception
simply because it is the necessary predicate of
everything conceivable.

Of course, if it is true that "everything

---

[66]*Ibid.*

[67]*Ibid.*

which can be conceptualized must have being," then
attributing being to anything one conceives becomes
tautological. For "being" is already involved in
every conception. But the most significant consequence of the notion that "being" is a universal
predicate is that it makes denials of the reality
of anything not readily intelligible. Indeed, in
the case of God, Tillich seems quite anxious to
make denials of God's being impossible. The fact
that Tillich believes he can, and does, deny God's
"existence"[68] is immaterial. For Tillich still
gives himself the option of talking about God's
"being," and otherwise implying that God nevertheless is, even in denials of his existence. This is
made perhaps most explicit in Tillich's claim that
the being of God is affirmed by the very act of
doubting him.[69] In fact, it turns out that God's
being is "implied in every statement about the relation between subject and predicate."[70] The problem is that what we mean to deny, when we deny
there is a God, is what Tillich means by God's being
—not simply his "existence." Tillich's denial that
God "exists," therefore, is gratuitous because he
has never given up God's being.

In sum, Tillich's notion of "being" simply by-
passes the necessity for any transition from concept

---

[68]ST I, p. 205.

[69]Tillich, "The Two Types of Philosophy of
Religion," p. 13.

[70]Ibid.

to reality. The bare thought of anything—including the thought of God in "the question of God"— is already objective. Thus, once Tillich identifies God as the "presupposition" of thought, God is no longer the object of that question but its objective basis.[71]

v

It remains to ask how the two general classes of concepts Tillich distinguishes within thinking "point to" the reality of being-itself. Tillich refers to these concepts, respectively, as "ontic" and "ontological."

An "ontic" concept, it has been suggested, is a "class" concept, since, according to Tillich, it is a concept that designates "a realm of beings."[72] An ontic concept, then, is simply the notion of an essence, since it has application to the several members of any given class of things. Tillich's example for such a concept is the essence "treehood."

"Ontological" concepts, on the other hand, are concepts which are more universal than ontic or class concepts, for they are universally predicable—that is, they are applicable to the members of every class. The reason ontological concepts are universally predicable is that they form part of the very structure of thinking itself. In this connection it might be noted that ontological con-

---

[71]*Ibid.*

[72]ST I, p. 164.

cepts are themselves comprised of two sub-groups:
the three pairs of "polar" elements, including "individuality" and "participation," and the categories of space, time, causality and substance. Now,
while ontological concepts are in some sense trans-
cendentals (i.e., universally predicable), they are,
all the same, still "less universal" than being-
itself,[73] which, according to Tillich, is fundamentally transcendental. That is, being-itself
must have application to every concept itself as
well as to any object, including those structures
of thought which are treated, analytically, as objects.

In any case, because both ontic and ontological concepts must possess "being," they are both,
in that way, objective. Thus, for Tillich, talking
about the concepts which form the various operations
of thinking at the same time tells us something
about the nature of objective reality.

How do ontic concepts "point to" the reality
of God? We have seen that ontic concepts, or essences, are real, since what they designate "is not
nothing" but possesses being. But it was also
pointed out that a concept must have form. Tillich
calls the "form" by which an essence has its being
the form of an "unactualized potential being." Before anything can come into actuality, in other
words, it must first have its being as something
potential. Moreover, Tillich emphasizes that this
is not one of mere logical possibility; it is a

---

[73]*Ibid.*

state of real being.[74]

Tillich sometimes characterizes the being of unactualized possibles as "relative non-being" or "not-yet-being."[75] This is misleading insofar as it implies that potentiality is a realm of "partial" being, of things "just emerging" into reality. In fact, the opposite is the case.

What Tillich in effect does is to associate a quasi-Platonic understanding of "existence" as the realm of imperfection, with the Christian doctrine of creation. Thus, coming into existence is understood to be an "estrangement" from the essential or perfect being in potentiality—a fall from essence to existence. Tillich argues that the existence of created things "stands out of their essence as in a 'fall.' On this point, the Platonic and the Christian evaluations of existence coincide."[76] Existence, from a religious point of view, is not a "perfection," but is a "falling away from what [something] essentially is...a loss of true essentiality."[77] It is the realm of opinion and error; it "lacks true reality."[78]

Consequently, the state of potentiality could hardly be a world of "half-real" beings. Rather,

---

[74] ST II, p. 20.

[75] *Ibid.*

[76] ST II, p. 23.

[77] ST II, p. 22.

[78] *Ibid.*

it is the realm of essences, of "true being," of
the "really real." "The potential is the essential,
and to exist...is the loss of true essentiality."[79]
Essential being is true being, and is present to us
in the form of the eternal essences, which are man's
"remembrances" of perfect being, "the essential
realm from which he fell into existence."[80]

Tillich implies that this realm of potentiality is also a divine one, that "essences are ideas
in the divine mind...the patterns according to
which God creates."[81] "The essential powers of
being belong to the divine life in which they are
rooted..."[82] What is significant about such remarks is that they suggest Tillich sees the "principle" that the potential is what is truly real as
a way of "pointing to" the reality of God. This
comes about, for Tillich, since claims about potentialities of human thought can also be understood as claims about God. For example, when Tillich talks about "the power of infinite self-transcendence [as] an expression of man's belonging to
that which is beyond being and nonbeing, namely, to
being-itself,"[83] this is also meant as an implicit
claim for the reality of being-itself. How? Because "the potential presence of the infinite (as

---

[79]*Ibid.*

[80]*Ibid.*

[81]ST I, p. 254.

[82]*Ibid.*

[83]ST I, p. 191.

unlimited self-transcendence)"[84] in us not only
"points to" the reality of being-itself. In fact,
it is a manifestation of being-itself: "Being-
itself manifests itself to finite being in the infinite drive of the finite beyond itself."[85]

Ontic concepts, then, appear to function as
a means for exhibiting the reality of God. There
are, of course, some problems Tillich's doctrine of
essences generates. For example, while Tillich
clearly wants to admit the reality of essences, he
is troubled about making them so individualized
that they become a mere "duplicate of reality."[86]
Yet it is just that idea of making essences into
individually existing things that Tillich himself
finds it impossible to avoid.

The problem originates in the very way Tillich states his doctrine that "being" is the basic
transcendental, the necessary predicate of everything conceivable. According to Tillich, being
"is the power in everything that has power, be it
a universal or an individual, a thing or an experience."[87]   But if it is the same being that is
predicated of both essences and individuals, then
there can be no distinction in reality between es-
ences and individuals. The consequence is that in

---

[84]*Ibid.*

[85]*Ibid.*

[86]ST I, p. 255.

[87]Tillich, "The Two Types of Philosophy of
Religion," p. 26.

talking about the ontological reality of essences,
Tillich finds it difficult to avoid referring to
essences as if they were, themselves, individually
existing things.

Tillich falls into this difficulty on at
least one occasion when he suggests that if all the
individuals of a given species should cease to exist, the form which constitutes the essence of that
species would still be "there," and, given the
right conditions, would come into actuality again:

> the potentialities of existence which we
> usually call the essences of things...have
> being, too; they are the power of being,
> which may become beings. For instance,
> even if suddenly a scourge should cause
> all trees to disappear, the tree, or the
> power of becoming a tree, would still be
> there; and given the right conditions, living
> trees might come into existence again.[88]

Now if all the individuals of a certain species of
tree should, for some reason, suddenly cease to be
(say, a blight) it is not only logically possible,[89]
but also, perhaps, a real possibility that individuals of that same species should one day reappear.[90]
Nevertheless, it is absurd to think they should
reappear for the reason that their "essence" is
still around. For even if it makes sense to speak
of the essence of an individual tree or of all the

---

[88]Brown, ed., *Ultimate Concern*, p. 45.

[89]In other words, in the sense that there is
nothing self-contradictory in the concept of a tree
that rules it out that there should be trees.

[90]For example, from some as yet unexplained
process of generation.

trees there are, there is not, in addition to those
trees, any entity designated by the word "treehood"
or "the tree"[91] and which exists after all those
individual trees have ceased to be. The essence
"treehood" which remains after all trees no longer
exist becomes just another possible individual tree,
eternally waiting in the wings, as it were, to make
its appearance.[92]

Now, what about the group of concepts Tillich
refers to as "ontological"? How do they also point
to the reality of God? According to Tillich, these
concepts constitute the conceptual structure

---

[91]Brown, ed., *Ultimate Concern*, p. 45.

[92]One of the strongest objections to entities
which are treated as "possible beings" is that it
seems impossible to provide any consistent criteria
of identity for them. If something, e.g., "the possible tree," is treated as a subject of which we can
make predications, it is necessary for it to be possible to tell in what circumstances two predications
are made of that same subject—lest we give up the
notion that contradictory predications cannot be
made of the same subject. Now while we have criteria by which we decide whether two statements are being made about the same actual tree, by what criteria
can we decide whether two statements are being made
about the same possible tree? How, for example, would
we decide whether "the possible male tree" and "the
possible spruce tree" are the same possible tree or
two? But if we can't decide that, then how can the
concept of identity be applied to "possible beings?"
Yet what sense can be made of talking of entities
which cannot meaningfully be said to be identical with
themselves and distinct from others. (Cf. Anthony
Kenny, *Descartes* [New York: Random House, 1968]), p.
168. Cf. also W. V. O. Quine, "On What There is," in
From a Logical Point of View, p. 4.

through which any experience is made intelligible, for ontological concepts are concepts of those "general structures that make experience possible."[93] These "structures, categories, and concepts which are presupposed in the cognitive encounter with every realm of reality,"[94] are "the forms in which the mind grasps and shapes reality."[95]

In a rough way Tillich's "ontological" concepts bear a certain resemblance to Kant's categories of the understanding.[96] In this sense "ontological" concepts are features of our subjective cognitive consittution; they are "in us," prior to experience. They relate to the general thesis that for experience to be possible at all, we must be able to experience things as falling under very general concepts which govern the operations of thinking.[97] They are "subjective" in the sense that they are those features of our cognition by which we actively order experience.[98]

---

[93]ST I, p. 19.

[94]ST I, p. 18.

[95]ST I, p. 192.

[96]Tillich notes (ST I, p. 166, n. 1) that space and time, which Kant had distinguished as the "forms of intuition," are assimilated under his own model of the categories of the understanding.

[97]Cf. P. F. Strawson, *The Bounds of Sense* (London: Methuen & Company, Ltd., 1966), p. 72.

[98]What Tillich means by the form by which the mind "shapes" reality.

But when Tillich calls these concepts "ontological," he clearly means to indicate that they
are not merely subjective. For ontological concepts are also said to be "the forms of being."[99]
"They are ontological...," and, according to Tillich, this means they are actually "present in
everything."[100]

In effect, Tillich is treating these ontological concepts, which constitute the elements
of the conceptual structure through which experience is actively ordered, as if they were properties of things. Unlike ontic concepts, essences
which determine things into classes, ontological
concepts are universally predicable of things of
every class. Nevertheless, they are, like essences,
objective—for they are actually "present in everything." Tillich reinforces this idea most strongly
when he identifies the ontological concepts which
constitute our cognitive structure as "the structural elements of being-itself."[101] What Tillich
has done, that is, is to identify the structure of
our cognition with God, who is the structure of objective reality. Tillich makes this quite explicit
when he states that God simply "*is* this structure"[102]
in terms of which our experience of the world is

---

[99]ST I, p. 192.

[100]*Ibid*.

[101]ST I, p. 238.

[102]ST I, pp. 238, 239, Tillich's emphasis.

ordered.

Now, if the concepts presupposed by thought
are identified as "the structural elements of being-
itself," then they are identical with that which
must have objective as well as subjective reality.
What Tillich appears to have accomplished, then,
is a way of talking about the nature of thinking
and the nature of God at the same time. For in
talking about those ontological concepts presupposed by thought, Tillich also takes himself to be
informing us about the nature of the ultimate
structure presupposed by thought: being-itself.

But if theology is thought about God, and God
is being-itself, the presupposition of all thought,
then the reality of God has simply become the presupposition of any theological inquiry.[103] By some
such move, that is, Tillich has established his own
form of ontological argument. We are justified in
referring to Tillich's procedure as a form of ontological argument precisely because the procedure is
an *a priori* one in the required sense. That is,
Tillich's analysis of God as being-itself, and the
relation of this concept to Tillich's understanding
of the nature of thinking, does not proceed from an
a posteriori investigation of our actual experience.
Rather, it is an *a priori* analysis of what must be
presupposed in order for there to be intelligible
experience at all. The reality of God, consequently,

---

[103]Cf. Stuart C. Brown, *Do Religious Claims
Make Sense?* (New York: The Macmillan Company, 1969),
p. 163.

becomes the presupposition of any possible epistemic theological inquiry, because, as being-itself,
God is simply identified with the presupposition
of the possibility of all thought. But from this
it follows that God cannot sensibly be the "object"
of any question about his existence, because God
must be its "basis." And that move, I take it, is
identical with Anselm's denial that it is possible
to conceive the non-existence of God. In Tillich's
case, it turns out that it is impossible to conceive the non-being of being-itself, since being-
itself is both present in, and the presupposition
of, any act of conceiving. What Tillich has done,
in effect, has been to recast the ontological argument in epistemic terms. Unfortunately, Tillich's
epistemology is far too laced with problems of its
own to consider his enterprise successful.

CHAPTER FOUR

PARADOX IN TILLICH'S THEOLOGY

The idea that theological explanations begin
and end in paradox is not unique to Tillich. Nevertheless, there is a radicalness to the manner in
which Tillich thinks certain paradoxes must be
stated which is a source of considerable perplex-
ity. The statement we have been considering in
these essays, "God does not exist," is the classic
example of a paradox of this sort. As the expression of a theologian it has the air of deliberate
paradox. At the same time, it is just this deliberateness which exemplifies Tillich's contention
that all attempts to conceptualize God are necessarily paradoxical.

Why does Tillich hold this thesis? In what
sense does the concept of God entail such paradoxes
in statements about him? In the course of examining this thesis, two important and related questions will have to be considered. (1) How does
Tillich distinguish paradox from flat contradiction,
and (2) why is Tillich forced to use the language
of paradox in order to say what presumably cannot
be illuminated in any other way? The first question will turn out to be another way of investi-
gating Tillich's criteria for meaning in theological assertions. The second will raise the often
obscured issue of the extent to which choice is

involved in the use of paradox. One is sometimes
urged to believe that assertions about religious
concepts necessitate paradox in the way that axioms
necessitate the falsity of their contraries. Tillich himself invites the idea that paradox is in
some way intrinsic to religion when he says that
"paradox is as necessary to every [theological] assertion as consistency is to every empirical scientific assertion."[1] Of course, if this were the
case, the meaning of those religious concepts could
not be at issue, since—on Tillich's analogy—the
paradox would arise only on the basis of complete
clarity of meaning conjoined to an impossible circumstance. In fact it is just because the meaning
of religious concepts is constantly at issue that
there is choice in the paradoxes they generate:
choice not only about whether to assert the paradox (vs. remaining silent, communicating in some
other way) but also choice about which paradox one
uses (since getting the right one determines the
range of possible responses). The necessity in religious paradox, then, is not one which obliterates
choice, but which places one's choices within exceedingly rigid logical boundaries. However, in
the case of Tillich's analysis of the concept of
God, these boundaries sometimes become so rigid
that it looks as if it's impossible to even hold
the concept, and this means that his attempt to

---

[1]Paul Tillich, "The Conquest of the Concept
of Religion in the Philosophy of Religion,"
p. 122.

distinguish between paradox and mere contradiction
will be put under considerable strain.

i

The question of the rigidity of boundaries in
assertions about God is perhaps the best place to
begin analysis of Tillich's understanding of paradox. It will also provide something of a clue to
the particular problems posed by Tillich's assertion "God does not exist." According to Tillich,
even "the word 'God' produces a contradiction in
the consciousness...."[2] What sort of a contradiction? When we try to hold the concept "God" in
thought, we are doing something...what? "Impossible" seems too strong because it implies the concept "God" itself is suspect—self-contradictory in
the way "round-square" is. What Tillich is worried
about, rather, has to do with the process of conceiving itself. Tillich explains as follows:

> ...it involves on the one hand something
> figurative that is a concrete object of
> the consciousness and on the other some-
> thing not figurative, something that is
> merely represented by this concrete ob-
> ject. The latter is what we really have
> in mind when we use the word "God."[3]

The "contradiction," then, seems to be based on
Tillich's notion that the term "God" (as well as

---

[2] Paul Tillich, *Religiöse Verwirklichung* (Berlin: Furche, 1929), cited in Adams, *Paul Tillich's
Philosophy of Culture, Science, and Religion*, p.
265.

[3] *Ibid*.

other terms substitutable for it) simultaneously
embodies two uses which are normally exclusive of
one another. (1) In its figurative sense, "God"
refers to some particular object—in general, a
person—about whom is asserted certain actions and
characteristics. Statements about God in this
sense are semantically identical to statements made
about you and me: as persons we do things, have
intentions, feelings, traits, etc. (2) However,
"God" also has a non-figurative sense for which
this object is a mere representation. It is in
this sense that "God" refers to unconditioned,
transcendent reality itself and with respect to
which the actions and qualities asserted of the object which "represents" it are negated, since this
being is not an object (i.e., it does not fall
under the Aristotelian category of substance, is
not a being).

Sometimes Tillich misleadingly suggests this
situation results from the word "God" having "a
double meaning"[4] which is surely false, since the
process of analysis which raises this issue is certainly not entailed by the meaning of the word
"God." Moreover, it is not entirely clear how this
situation is one of "contradiction." Tillich's
suggestion that it is largely rests on his claim
to the simultaneity of the term's functioning as a
genuine representation and as a mere representation,

---

[4]Paul Tillich, "The Religious Symbol," in
Hook, ed., *Religious Experience and Truth*, p.
315.

of having a non-figurative and a figurative sense.
"In the word 'God' is contained at the same time
that which actually functions as a representation
and also the idea that it is only a representation."[5]

Now many terms have both figurative and non-
figurative senses (e.g., "the Sun") but they are
not used simultaneously, as Tillich claims in the
case with "God." Also, the way the contrast between figurative and non-figurative customarily occurs is quite different in the case of "God." For
example, "the Sun" figuratively refers to Juliet,
non-figuratively to a celestial object. So the
contrast here is between one object and another—
or one category of object (inanimate) and another
(personal). But while "God" figuratively refers
to an object before one's consciousness (e.g., a
divine perfect person), non-figuratively it refers
to something that is not an object at all (unconditioned reality). Furthermore, while one is free to
use "the Sun" to refer to either Juliet or a celestial body, one is not free to exercise that choice
with "God" because the logical strictures governing
its use require that it be both sides of the con-
trasting senses at once. (This does not mean, however, that there is no choice in the contrasts "God"
generates, as I will subsequently show.)

Thus, the nature of the "contradiction" the
term "God" produces seems to be as follows. (1) It

---

[5]*Ibid.*

is a result of a process of conceiving which arises
in the use of the term, rather than from the meaning of the term itself (although Tillich is not always clear on this point). (2) This process of
conceiving God elicits a simultaneity of figurative
and non-figurative senses in the use of "God."
(3) The peculiarity of the contrast between the
figurative and non-figurative senses of "God" is
its reference, respectively, to an object vs. something that is not an object.

     Tillich describes this last aspect of the
"contradiction in one's consciousness" as "the peculiarity of ["God"] transcending its own conceptual
content."[6] What this "transcending" seems to involve is a negating of the objectivity present in
the figurative sense of the term "God." Unfortunately, the precise meaning of this process of negating remains ambiguous because Tillich fails to
distinguish between at least two things it might
possibly entail. Negating the objective character
of "God"—i.e., negating those predicates which assert actions, intentions, qualities, etc. of him—
could mean (a) that such predicates do not apply to
God in their ordinary way, or (b) that those predicates do not apply at all.

     In the former, Tillich would be saying that
there is no meaningful sense in which predicates
ascribing actions, intentions, qualities, etc. can
be applied to God when "God" is understood in its
non-figurative (i.e., non-objective) sense. In
this case, however, Tillich would be committing himself to the unavailability of any meaningful asser-

---

[6] *Ibid.*

tion about God, and that raises considerable difficulties if one wants to affirm God's existence.
Unfortunately, Tillich often seems quite ready to
deny one can do that, although, as I have suggested
elsewhere in these essays, to take his statement
"God does not exist" univocally would clearly be to
take it a step further than Tillich intends.

The problem in making sense out of what Tillich means by "negating this objectivity" is that
he seems to vacillate between both of these possible interpretations. At the same time, it is crucial to try to make some sense of it because the
issue of Tillich's purported atheism turns on it in
a number of important ways, as the following passage shows:

> ...theory makes the Unconditional into an
> object, i.e., precisely what it is not.
>
> ...every actuality exists in the forms of
> objectivity, of which one is existence it-
> self. At the same time, however, within
> every actuality there is something uncondi-
> tionally real to be grasped. This uncondi-
> tionally real is not defined by the forms
> of objects and has, therefore, likewise no
> existence. Where the spirit directs itself
> upon the world and its contents in such a
> way that it brings to awareness the im-
> pulse of unconditionality implicit in all
> things, there it is directed toward God.
> This power of unconditional reality in every
> conditioned actuality is that which is the
> supporting ground in every thing (Ding), its
> very root of being, its absolute seriousness,
> its unfathomable depth, and its holiness.
> It is the import of its reality as distin-
> guished from its accidental form.
>
> All objective thinking must be strictly ex-
> cluded here. We are not dealing with an
> object to be found either alongside things,

> or above or within them. The material
> objective (*Gegenständlichen*) is not under
> consideration here at all, but rather the
> primordial (*Urständlichen*) as such, that
> which is exempt from all form, including
> that of existence. But here again it is
> the case that every statement is expressed
> in a material-objective form, and therefore
> is true only as a broken, paradoxical
> statement.
>
> Thus, in respect to its form the statement
> "God is" is theoretical. No classifica-
> tion according to levels can change this,
> since God is thereby brought into the order
> of the world of objects. This pigeon-holing
> of God, however, is atheism. If the state-
> ment "God is" is likewise theoretical in its
> import, then it destroys the divinity of God.
> Meant as paradox, however, it is the neces-
> sary expression for the affirmation of the
> Unconditional, for it is not possible to
> direct oneself toward the Unconditional
> apart from objectification.[7]

Even exempting the problem of giving content——religious or otherwise——to the notion of "the unconditionally real within every actuality" which Tillich identifies with God,[8] it is hard to see how
any content can be given to "that which is exempt
from all form." Yet Tillich always expresses himself in a way which forces one to fall short of
simply identifying God with sheer undifferentiated
formlessness. Consider the following formulations:

> (1) Theory makes the Unconditional into an
>   object, i.e., precisely what it is not.

---

[7]Tillich, "The Conquest of the Concept of Religion in the Philosophy of Religion," pp. 140-141.

[8]This is discussed in "God and Singular Existence" and "The 'Non-Existence' of God."

(2) The unconditionally real is not defined
     by the forms of objects.

(3) All objective thinking must be strictly
     excluded here.

(4) The primordial as such—that which is
     exempt from all form.

Each of these at least gives hints which tell us
something about why the process of conceiving "God"
is a paradoxical one. With the first, we know
(from Freudian psychology, for example) what it is
for a theory to make something into an object which
is not an object. In (2) we know that, for example,
numbers are "not defined" by the forms of objects—
indeed are not defined at all. The third is somewhat trickier because it is the recognition of an
attitude—excluding—about something as broad and
loose as "objective thinking." The "trickiness"
arises because the recognition of an attitude
clearly allows for the possibility of its alternatives: i.e., I can only work at excluding one sort
of thinking because it is always possible for its
opposite to creep back in. The kind of example
which comes to mind here is one of the advice typically given to the yogin initiate about the objects of his concentration.

     With (4) it seems arguable, at least, that
Tillich has gone over the border of intelligibility
(i.e., of that which is without form we must be
silent). But a sympathetic reading might distinguish between "exempt from" and "without" form, allowing that with the former one is being advised,
in a manner similar to (3), to treat statements

about God expressed "in a material-objective form" as necessarily paradoxical.

At this point we have not progressed much beyond the stage of hints in our understanding of what Tillich means in saying the process of conceiving God is a paradoxical one, because while pointing out that the statements we make about God in a material-objective form are paradoxical may be symptomatic of the "contradiction in our consciousness," it is not the same thing as it. Indeed, one might have a quite clear conception of something that can only be expressed in paradoxical statements.

While Tillich is concerned about the things we can say about God, he is more concerned with what we can think apart from saying (which is one reason Tillich's theology is so resistant to analysis by linguistic philosophy). Surely it is more than a worry about language that leads Tillich to make a connection between the sense in which conceiving God is conceiving of something "exempt from all form" and his claim that "God does not exist." The reason is simply that the statement "God does not exist" is inconsistent with the position of one who otherwise clearly affirms there is a God, and therefore in making the statement "God does not exist," Tillich must have gone beyond the concerns of language. The unfortunate connection between the inability to conceive of God under the category of any form and Tillich's purported atheism appears at a number of points in the passage we have been considering.

Since Tillich regards "existence" as one of the "forms of objectivity" in which every actuality exists, it would appear he considers "exists" as a logical predicate. At least that seems to be the most straightforward way to understand his remark that unconditioned reality, which is not defined by the forms of objects, therefore has no existence. The claim that God is not defined by, or is exempt from, all form, is Tillich's restatement of Aquinas' doctrine that God transcends all genera.[9] But unlike the consequence of that doctrine, Tillich is not satisfied to see God understood as an abstraction, the most universal of all concepts. Therefore, God is identified with the primordial depth of holiness of everything. But even this attempt to suggest a religious content for the notion of the unconditionally real implicit in all things still makes use of "material-objective" categories and therefore "represents" God as an object. For that reason Tillich allows that those statements are only paradoxically true.

The deliberateness of the paradox Tillich claims is necessarily present in our conceiving God is most patent in his withholding the application of existence to God. Some confusion is generated just because when Tillich urges that there is an atheism necessarily present in any theological statement about God[10] in which God is brought into

---

[9] Aquinas, *Summa Theologiae* IA. Q3, art. 6, reply to obj. 2.

[10] ST I, p. 245 and Tillich, "The Two Types

"the world of objects," this is not the same sense
of "atheism" which follows from withholding the
application of existence to God. From withholding
the application of existence to God it follows that
there is no God. We can call this the standard
sense of atheism, because it is the sense which
differentiates the atheist from the believer. From
Tillich's sense of "atheism," however, it clearly
does not follow that there is no God (that is, the
atheist and believer are not differentiated), but
only that God has been conceived—"pigeon-holed"—
under the order of the world of objects. At the
same time, Tillich conflates these two senses of
atheism by treating "exists" as a logical predicate.
Therefore, applying the concept of existence to God
is also conceiving of God as an object. Hence we
can see why Tillich regards all affirmations of
God's existence as "atheistic."[11] In asserting
God's existence, according to Tillich, we must
necessarily conceive of God as an object. But as
the unconditionally real, God is not an object.
For that reason we cannot—except paradoxically—
assert God's existence. "God is" can only be a
genuine affirmation of God if it is understood as
a "broken, paradoxical statement." "Broken" can

---

of Philosophy of Religion,", p. 25.

[11]ST I, p. 237.

be understood in the double sense of (a) the failure of any form to adequately express the reality
it seeks to deliver, and (b) the breaking through
of that reality despite the inadequacy of its forms
of representation.

The "atheism" which Tillich sees as necessarily present in any religious affirmation of God is
therefore not meant as a denial of the reality of
that which is intuited in the religious symbols
used to express that affirmation. Rather, "atheism," as Tillich employs it, might be said to be
the form of representing God. The appropriateness
of saying this should be apparent insofar as one
can see that (a) any "representation" of God necessarily leads one away from that which is represented, but (b) the reality of that which cannot be
represented breaks through that contradiction in
the consciousness anyway.

As J. L. Adams, Tillich's best-known interpre-
ter, suggests, Tillich's "atheism"

> ...is rather a denial of the theoretical con-
> ception that uses the principle of analogy as
> a basis for rational construction whereby God
> or the Unconditioned is made into an object.
> A god who is a being behind the world or who
> is a probable hypothesis cannot be of ultimate
> concern. Such a view of deity is not so much
> false as it is a distortion. "Atheism" is a
> protest against this distortion. It is an
> implicit affirmation of the Unconditioned as
> a qualification of existence and a denial
> that the Unconditioned is one element among
> others. It is an implicit affirmation of the
> paradoxical character of the immanence of the
> transcendent.[12]

---

[12]Adams, *op. cit.*, p. 248.

There is a distinctly Kantian undertone to the
suggestion of Tillich's "denial of theoretical
conceptions" of God. God cannot be made an object
of theoretical knowledge, and since Tillich regards
the existential statement "God is" as formally theoretical,[13] Tillich places the bare affirmation of
the existence of God under the strain normally re-
served for claims of knowledge of God.[14] However,
unlike Kant, Tillich cannot conclude that any "experience of God" is therefore impossible, because
it is the very purpose of "the protest of atheism"
(in Tillich's sense of "atheism") to affirm that
God must—if we are to speak of God at all—be a
matter of ultimate, personal concern. It is to affirm, that is, the "immanence of the transcendent."

   Tillich is not, however, writing out of the
experience of any particular tradition, nor is he
suggesting that God must be the object of some particular religious experience. Rather, he is attempting to develop—in a somewhat oblique way—
part of the logic of the concept of God from which
it follows that God must be the subject of some
possible experience. For this reason, it would not
be inaccurate to maintain that Tillich regards it

---

[13]Tillich, "The Conquest of the Concept of
Religion in the Philosophy of Religion," p. 141.

[14]For Aquinas we have no knowledge of God in
this life other than by analogy, except for our
ability to demonstrate (1) that God exists and (2)
that God's essence and existence are identical.
For Tillich we cannot have knowledge of even these
two propositions, nor can we assert them non-para-
doxically.

as the mark of any serious theology (i.e., theology that does not give us what he calls a "distortion" of God) that it is necessarily experiential.

At the same time, it is also this circumstance which gives theology its necessarily paradoxical character. A general formulation of the paradox which pervades Tillich's theology may be expressed in terms of the following three theses:

    (1)   The experience of every actuality occurs under some form of objectivity.

    (2)   As unconditioned reality, God is not an object. (The "unconditionally real is not defined by the forms of objects.")[15]

    (3)   As our ultimate concern, God is a possible object of experience. ("It is not possible to direct oneself toward the Unconditional apart from objectification.")[16]

As they stand, these statements form a logically inconsistent triad. Not surprisingly, however, Tillich attempts to turn this apparent dilemma into a tour de force by distinguishing between logical contradiction and religious paradox. Unlike logical paradoxes, Tillich believes that religious paradoxes are ultimately unresolvable, and it is this feature which defines the context for any possible theological assertion:

---

[15]Tillich, "The Conquest of the Concept of Religion in the Philosophy of Religion," p. 140.

[16]*Ibid.*, p. 141; see also p. 139 and ST I, pp. 172-3 on "object."

> ...every statement about the Unconditional
> is necessarily in the form of a paradox.
> Aesthetic and logical paradoxes are in
> principle resolvable. Both present a prob-
> lem to be solved, either by common sense or
> by logical thought. But the paradox of the
> Unconditional is not resolvable.[17]

A number of things about this distinction need to be said. In the first place, Tillich consistently maintains that Christian users of paradox in general do "not intend to say something illogical."[18] Indeed, more than that

> Paradox in religion and theology does not
> conflict with the principle of logical
> rationality. Paradox has its logical
> place.[19]

Given Tillich's analysis of God as unconditioned being, and the theses that analysis generates, one can see why Tillich comes to the view that paradox is endemic to theology, and therefore unresolvable. The question which remains, however, is how he can consistently maintain that (1) religious paradoxes are not in principle resolvable, and (2) they do not conflict with the principle of logical rationality.

Part of the reason Tillich thinks he can is that while the problematical character of religious paradox is given a certain rhetorical force over logical contradiction by being called "in principle unresolvable," Tillich's definition of paradox

---

[17]*Ibid.*, p. 123.

[18]ST I, p. 56.

[19]ST I, p. 57.

turns out to be considerably weaker than one
might expect.

> The term 'paradox' should be defined care-
> fully, and paradoxical language should be
> used with discrimination. Paradoxical
> means 'against the opinion,' namely, the
> opinion of finite reason. Paradox points
> to the fact that in God's acting finite
> reason is superseded but not annihilated;
> it expresses the fact in terms which are
> not logically contradictory but which are
> supposed to point beyond the realm in which
> finite reason is applicable.[20]

What is apparent is that Tillich has removed the
"conflict" between religious paradox and the principle of logical rationality by reducing logic to
a "set of opinions" which must be superseded. The
only justification for this seems to be that logic
is "finite" and inapplicable to the divine "realm."
But what calling logic "finite" masks is the fact
that if a statement is logically contradictory, it
is so because it is internally inconsistent, not
because it is "finite."

Now Tillich is not suggesting that statements about God which are internally inconsistent
suddenly, because God is their subject, become co-
herent in some "higher" way. We are not, he says,
"asked to sacrifice reason in order to accept
senseless combinations of words as divine wisdom."[21]
At the same time he implies there is some higher
order of reason—the specific nature of whose paradox remains unclear—which becomes manifest to us

---

[20]*Ibid.*

[21]*Ibid.*

in our experience.

> ...the acceptance of this paradox is not
> the acceptance of the absurd, but it is
> the state of being grasped by the power
> of that which breaks into our experience
> from above it.[22]

Unfortunately, the shift to claims about the possibilities of our experience does nothing to clarify
the conceptual distinction Tillich wants to make
between religious paradox and logical contradiction. Consequently, his insistence that the religious paradoxes are not in conflict with the
principle of logical rationality remains unsupport-
ed.

ii

The deliberately paradoxical character which
permeates Tillich's theology derives from his
analysis of the concept of God, a predominant feature of which is to urge that God must be conceived
as the Unconditioned, or Being-itself, over against
the concept of God as a person. It is the error
of "ordinary theism," Tillich argues, to have "made
God a heavenly, completely perfect person who re-
sides above the world and mankind."[23] The correc-
tive to that error is to acknowledge that "God is
being-itself, not a being."[24] However, it is just
that formulation which produces the paradox of any

---

[22]*Ibid*.

[23]ST I, p. 245.

[24]ST I, p. 237.

attempt in representing God, since "man cannot be
ultimately concerned about anything that is less
than personal."[25]

From Tillich's worries about "ordinary theism," it is easy to draw the conclusion that the
concepts of a personal God and unconditioned being
stand in polar contrast with one another and that
the deliberateness of the paradox in Tillich's theology results from his insistence on holding these
two opposing notions together. In fact, it is al-
most the opposite that is the case. That is,
Tillich sees the notion of unconditioned being as
precisely what it takes to express the idea of a
personal God so utterly and intimately related to
the world that Tillich refers to him as the "absolute participant."[26] "Unconditioned being" is in
one important respect a misleading term, for it
implies Tillich's concept of God is altogether non-
personal—an abstraction. How could one pray to
being-itself, for example?

But it is simply not the case that Tillich's
notion of God as being-itself is non-personal.
What is difficult is to show that it is not. I am
not satisfied that Tillich gets very far in trying
to do that, despite his claims that being-itself,
when taken as the basic *transcendentale* (or power
of being), is not the emptiest but "the most mean-

---

[25]ST I, p. 244.

[26]*Ibid.*

ingful of all concepts."[27] What is more useful,
I think, is to indicate why Tillich thinks it
takes the concept of unconditioned being to properly express the notion of a personal God. One sees
Tillich struggling to do this especially in *Biblical Religion and the Search for Ultimate Reality,*
where he argues that the notions of "being-itself"
and "person" are not incompatible:

> ...the God who is a person is transcended
> by the God who is the Personal-Itself...
>
> ...*being* and *person* are not contradictory
> concepts. Being includes personal being;
> it does not deny it. The ground of being
> is the ground of personal being, not its
> negation...
>
> Religiously speaking...our encounter with
> the God who is a person includes the en-
> counter with the God who is the ground of
> everything personal and as such not *a*
> person.[28]

Embodied in this analysis are two notions of
"person" which need to be distinguished because
only one of them is regarded by Tillich as predicable of God. The distinction depends on an associa-
tion of one use of the concept of "person" with the
idea of participation or communality. God cannot
be called "a person," according to Tillich, because
anything which falls under the category of substance (individuality) must be ontologically separate from every other substance. God, however, is

---

[27] ST II, p. 11.

[28] Tillich, *Biblical Religion and the Search
for Ultimate Reality,* pp. 82-83.

not ontologically separate from any substance, as
the concept of being-itself (or ground of being)
as the absolute participant is meant to imply. In
terms of our experience, "the divine life participates in every life as its ground and aim. God
participates in everything that is; he has community with it."[29]

For Tillich, the fundamental philosophico-
theological problem is that what gets called God
in religion is not, after all, God. If what one
worships is conceived as some super-existing individual of infinite power and infinite duration, who
controls the universe, then that—from Tillich's
standpoint—might as well not exist, for such a
being could not be a matter of ultimate concern.
Why does Tillich think this?

Tillich's reasons are never made explicit,
but one can extrapolate a number of suggestions
from remarks Tillich makes against the possibility
of producing empirical evidence for God's existence. In Tillich's view, the concept of anything
which is an individual substance—a particular being—is the concept of something that falls under
the domain of scientific investigation and for
which evidence is relevant to establish its existence. The "error" of ordinary theism is to think
it can make God secure from empirical investigation by claiming God to have certain "perfections"
—properties in a superlative degree. If God were

---

[29]ST I, p. 245.

such a being it would first of all be false that
he exists since no evidence for his existence has
ever been produced.[30]   Moreover, no individual substance can be freed from empirical limitation simply by possessing properties in an infinite degree.
This seems to be what Tillich has in mind when he
says such a concept of God "brings God's existence
down to the level of that of a stone or a star."[31]
Possessing infinite power does not itself free a
substance from causal conditions, for example; some
additional argument would be needed for that (and
would have to be made to distinguish "God" from an
infinitely powerful material substance).

Finally, Tillich denies that such a "highest
being" could be a matter of ultimate concern for
us[32] even if it existed. It is perhaps this view
of Tillich's which, I think, is hardest to comprehend. Each of us has had the experience of concern
for some other individual, and each of us can probably imagine a being whose concern for us would be
infinite—who could protect us, defend us from evil,
sustain our existence, etc. Now it must be emphasized that Tillich is not worried about the concrete
content of our "concern" because the issue for him
is not one of anthropomorphism. Tillich, that is,

---

[30]Tillich, "The Idea of God as Affected by
Modern Knowledge," 85; ST I, p. 245.

[31]Tillich, "The Two Types of Philosophy of
Religion," p. 18.

[32]ST I, p. 245.

is not worried about the humanness of our concerns.
Because God is personal, our "concern" is personal.
"Anthropomorphic symbols are adequate for speaking
of God religiously. Only in this way can he be
the living God for man."[33] Anthropomorphic symbols
cannot represent (i.e., in the sense of "resemble")
being-itself. (Nothing can.) But they can "refer
to "being-itself and thereby give the concept religious significance. For this reason, even the term
"highest being" can function as "a symbol for that
which is not symbolic in the idea of God—namely,
'Being Itself.'"[34]

Tillich's worry in denying God is a person
that is not that the concepts of "person" and "being-itself" are incompatible. Tillich argues they
are not. Nor is it that being-itself cannot properly be referred to as an object of our concern. It
can, through religious symbols. Tillich's worry,
rather, is that a person cannot be the object of
ultimate concern, since ultimate concern cannot be
experienced if there is any ontological separation
between the object of concern and ourselves. This
is surely the intent behind Tillich's frequent en-
dorsement of Luther's remark that God is nearer to
us than we are to ourselves.[35]

---

[33]ST I, p. 242.

[34]Paul Tillich, "The Nature of Religious Language," in *Theology of Culture, op. cit.*, p. 61.

[35]Paul Tillich, "Escape From God," in *The
Shaking of the Foundations*, p. 44.

I don't claim that the meaning of that remark, or of the idea behind it, is entirely clear
—although I feel confident that it is intelligible.
But clear or not, I do think it commits Tillich to
the position where the experience of God must be
understood to unfold as an experience of ourselves.
That is, what is peculiar to Tillich's analysis of
that experience is that we are somehow present in
it as its content. If "the divine life participates in every life as its ground and aim," and if
participation involving relationships of ultimate
concern entails the absence of all ontological separation between the participants, then in an important sense we are identical with God at the same
time that God infinitely transcends the world.
That paradox—the paradox of God's simultaneous
transcendence of the world and immanence to everything in it—is clearly the predominant feature of
Tillich's theology.[36] Moreover, it is his insistence that this paradox is intrinsic to the concept
of God that makes any attempt to conceptualize God
a correspondingly paradoxical process—one which
Tillich ultimately regards it as of no use to try
to remove.

iii

I have suggested that the most interesting
but problematic feature of Tillich's theology is
his suggestion that the concept of unconditioned

---

[36]Cf. Adams, *op. cit.*, p. 155.

being, or being-itself, is required in order for
us to properly understand how God can be personal
—viz., in the sense in which there can be no ontological separation between man and that which is
his ultimate concern. This is problematic because
the concept of being-itself is generally taken to
be highly abstract and therefore impersonal. For
this reason it is frequently proposed that Tillich
wants to replace the concept of a personal God
with that of impersonal Being. But this simply
misses the fact that Tillich is making use of an
abstract concept to refer to a personal God, with
whom, despite the abstraction, our relation is
primarily experiential.

According to Lewis Ford, for example, the
mistake in Tillich's polemic against the idea that
God is a being is that Tillich winds up denying
the God of the Judeo-Christian tradition in favor
of "the unconditioned, impersonal Brahma of Hindu-
ism."[37] But this is not correct. As I argued in
"God and Singular Existence," Tillich's claim that
God is not a being sometimes leads to the confusion
that God could be a property of everything—what
seems implied when Tillich says, for example, that
being-itself is a quality of everything that is[38]

---

[37]Lewis S. Ford, "Tillich and Thomas: The
Analogy of Being." *The Journal of Religion*, XLVI,
No. 2 (April, 1966), 243.

[38]Paul Tillich, "The Meaning and Justification of Religious Symbols," in Hook, *op. cit.*, p. 7.

or the "power inherent in everything."[39] However, this is not the error which is involved in the suggestion that Tillich has "replaced" one concept of God with another. Tillich's problems arise out of his own analysis of the concept of being-itself. But the criticism which sees Tillich wanting to devoid the idea of the personal God of the Bible of all content in favor of a concept so abstract and empty that Tillich winds up regarding God as an impersonal Nothing incorrectly assumes Tillich's view of the solution to theological paradox is simply to replace one paradox with another. It assumes Tillich is satisfied with having reached a conception of God which is at a sufficient level of abstraction to avoid the idea that God is a particular, individual substance.

But not only does this misconstrue what Tillich's intention is in using the abstract notion of being-itself, it fails to capture what his initial worry was. That worry has something to do with Tillich's belief that any representation of something gets in the way of the experience of that thing, just as much as it makes the thing available. Thus, it is not as if Tillich wants to replace the biblical picture of a personal God with another picture—that of an impersonal Nothing. What Tillich wants is for those pictures to drop off altogether.

Tillich's worry has fundamentally two aspects.

---

[39]ST I, p. 236.

(1) Formally, it is that any concept or symbol
used to characterize God should itself become the
object of our ultimate concern.[40]   (2) Materially,
it is that a certain standard way (i.e., ordinary
theism) of conceiving what a person is necessarily
falsifies how our personal relation to God must be
understood. The first emphasizes the sense in
which we are not free to avoid the paradox generated, according to Tillich, in any theological assertion about God. The second emphasizes the sense
in which some choice in what we can say is nevertheless retained. The first lays out the boundaries of meaningfulness of assertions using religious
concepts. The second represents the attempt to
provide the content to those theological assertions
whose formal properties (viz., that any symbol
could become our object of ultimate concern instead
of God) appear to contradict that they could have
any meaning. That is, if no concept can non-para-
doxically represent God because the concrete content of that concept stands as a potential barrier
in referring to God, then one might be strongly
tempted to say the concept of God must itself be
self-contradictory. That, however, is a position
Tillich surely does not occupy.

Let me say something further about each of
these. (1) With regard to the formal properties
that attend any theological assertion and which
render it paradoxical, it is, in a sense, Tillich's

---

[40]Cf. ST I, p. 44.

extreme realism[41]——the idea that "being" belongs
to every conceivable term[42]——that makes this problem a real one. That is, there is no sense in
which any paradox about God can be simply a formal
one. This is the strain his entire theory of symbolic language is under. Every statement about
God (other than "God is being-itself") is symbolic
——a mere representation of that which cannot be
represented. Yet it can never be just a mere representation either in the following sense. Since
"being" is possessed by every conceivable term, and
God is being-itself, then every statement about God
ultimately participates in the reality to which it
purportedly only "symbolically" refers. This is
why Tillich is so curiously concerned about the
idea that we might "mistake" the symbols we use to
represent God for God himself: because every symbol
is still ontologically linked to God through a common being Tillich insists is shared by everything,
which is inherent in everything. Of course, if
God is being-itself, this has the advantage of
making any symbolic statement give some sort of access to God, although not by what we ordinarily
take to be the content of that symbolic statement.
The access, rather, is by the purely formal property——being——the symbol possesses. It is for just
this reason that Tillich is sometimes led to suggest that any statement about anything can be

---

[41]See all the discussion in "A Form of Ontological Argument."

[42]ST I, p. 179.

informative about God.[43]

Whether we should view this situation as one
that makes the concept of God, as being-itself,
extraordinarily rich or absolutely empty seems to
be largely a matter of taste. That is, one can
consider the notion of "being" and imagine an in-
finitude of permutations of being—an infinite
number of life stories, as it were. But one can
just as easily consider the notion of "being" as
bare, undifferentiated (and, therefore, content-
less) reality. Intuitively, I am inclined to think
it makes some sense to speak of the "experience" of
the fullness of being on the one hand, and the "con-
templation"of bare reality on the other, and that
it is significant that the possibilities of enter-
taining the concept of "being" divide themselves
in this way. Moreover (and also intuitively), I
think these two possibilities complement one another rather than contradict each other. However, I
also think it should be quite hard, if not impossible, to show that this is the case.

In any case, the formal paradox Tillich believes is necessarily part of any attempt to conceive God is the one which entails that any picture
we have of God can only lead us away from God. Thus,
for Tillich, the idea of getting rid of a "bad"
picture and replacing it with another "better" one
ultimately brings us no further along. For one

---

[43]Tillich, "The Two Types of Philosophy of
Religion," p. 13; Cf. also ST I, p. 188: being-
itself "means being everything" and ST I, p. 179.

cannot remove the paradox which is necessarily a part of any thought of God; one can only alter its appearance.

When Tillich remarks that the word God produces a contradiction in our consciousness, he means (a) that to speak of God we must make some concrete representation. That is, when we use the word "God," a picture—some picture—must appear before the mind, as it were, if we are to think of God at all; (b) yet no picture can represent God. For what we mean by God is none of those pictures. It is in that sense that the meaning of religious concepts is always at issue. This is not the same, however, as saying that if God is not the absolute, personal Something then he must be the absolute, impersonal Nothing.[44] Nor is it the same as saying "there is no God." The former assumes we have the criteria so that when we know one picture is the wrong one, we also know when another is the right one—precisely what Tillich denies we can have. The latter goes a step further, on the assumption that if there can be no way to have the right picture of God, then the notion of "God" must be self-contradictory and, therefore, unintelligible—a position, I have argued, Tillich surely does not occupy. Thus, for Tillich, God is not one (an absolute Something) or the other (an absolute Nothing),

[44] Paul Tillich, "Ueber die Idee einer Theologie der Kultur," in *Religionsphilosophie der Kultur; Zwei Entwürfe von Gustav Radbruch und Paul Tillich* (Berlin: Reuther und Reichard, 1919), p. 35, quoted in Adams, *op. cit.*, pp. 43-44.

but rather neither (no picture is correct) or, as
the Super-existing[45] (the being which transcends
all conceptual distinctions), simultaneously both.

(2) What, then, about the material properties of theological assertions? While no picture
can represent God, "having" a picture of God is
not a dispensable feature of theology; nor is it
necessarily a bad one. This is the point at which,
within the logical boundaries for any theological
assertion, the believer exercises choice over his
manner of conceiving God. That choice, however,
is not without certain conditions.

In the first place, the picture we do have
is important because it determines the outward
form of religion: the nature of belief and religious praxis. If theology is to speak of God at
all, it must make of God some concrete representation, some object, or symbol, which, according to
Tillich, "points to" its infinite subject although
it is itself a finite something, since it is the
object of our thought. However, insofar as "God"
is something we conceive, something of which we
have some conception, we are not simply free to
use that "something" in any way we please. Rather,
depending on the way in which God is "there" for
us, the picture we have tells us what we must believe. For the nature of that concrete concept of
God is what determines the nature and possibilities
of our religious experience. As Tillich says, it

---

[45]*Ibid.*

is because "the ultimate can become actual only
through the concrete" that "the idea of God has a
history."[46] In this way, Tillich's historical
typology of concepts of God (universalistic, myth-
ological and dualistic polytheism; monarchic,
mystical, exclusive and trinitarian monotheism)[47]
can be seen as defining the possibilities of religious experience each of those concepts entails.
While one may, in a limited sense, be free to
choose among them (e.g., by conversion or contingent historical change), the possibilities of one's
experience within each of those concepts are determined, with varying degrees of rigidity, by features intrinsic to that concept.

It should be emphasized that what I am talking about here is the conceptual relation between
a concept and the possibilities of experience under
it, and not the question of whether one's concept
of God is determined by his experience or vice
versa. The point is that, given a certain concept
of God, only certain kinds of religious experience
will be consistent with it. For example, the possibility of competing lóci of divine powers arises
in universalistic polytheism, but not in exclusive
monotheism. Or again, to see one's experience of
reality defined in terms of "the conflict between
divine and demonic holiness"[48] (dualistic poly-

---

[46]ST I, p. 218.

[47]ST I, p. 218 ff.

[48]ST I, p. 224.

theism) constitutes a perception quite different from that determined by the concept of "the god-monarch [who] rules over the heirarchy of inferior gods."[49] In the former, man has the status of a co-worker with the power of divine goodness in a cosmic battle, while in the latter, he is a mere supplicant for divine protection. Those percep-tions of reality are as different as the percep-tions of a field marshall and a private of the same war. It is in this way that the concrete picture we have of God can determine the entire texture of our lives.

In the second place, as I have indicated, Tillich does not at all think that "having a pic-ture" of God is bad—even if we could somehow "es-cape" from having one. We have seen, for example, that Tillich regards the symbol "personal God" as essential for religious experience, and that from God's not being a person, it does not follow that we cannot regard God as personal. "'Personal God' does not mean that God is a person. It means that God is the ground of everything personal.... He is not a person, but he is not less than personal."[50]

Why is this picture not a dispensible fea-ture of theology? In genuine theological assertions

---

[49]ST I, pp. 225-26.

[50]ST I, p. 245. From God's not being a per-son, Tillich does not, for example, find it incon-ceivable that we should pray to God. See, e.g., Paul Tillich, "The Concept of God," *Perspective*, Vol. II, No. 3 (January, 1950), 12: "The believer can pray to the 'personal' God whom he faces...."

according to Tillich, "the symbol 'personal God'
is absolutely fundamental because an existential
relation is a person-to-person relation."[51] But
the criterion of genuine theological assertions is
to have this "existential" character.[52] Such assertions are ones whose object "is a matter of infinite passion"[53] for us. "Only those propositions
are theological which deal with their object insofar as it can become a matter of ultimate concern
for us."[54] And since "man cannot be ultimately
concerned about anything that is less than personal,"[55] it follows that genuine theological assertions—ones which express "ultimacy"—must employ
the symbol "personal God." Indeed, "the personal
encounter with God and reunion with him are the
heart of all genuine religion."[56]

Tillich's unease about God being an individual being—a person—is that, while it is conceivable that one person can remain external, unrelated

---

[51]ST I, p. 244. See also Paul Tillich "Science and Theology: A Discussion with Einstein" in
Theology of Culture, op. cit., p. 132 where Tillich
refers to Schelling: "'Only a person can heal a
person.' This is the reason that the symbol of the
Personal God is indispensible for living religion."

[52]ST I, p. 12.

[53]*Ibid.*

[54]*Ibid.*

[55]ST I, p. 244.

[56]ST II, p. 86.

to another, it is inconceivable that God should
not be related to (i.e., love) the world. The
problem is not simply that Tillich thinks a certain
conception of God as a "heavenly person"makes God
into a finite being. The problem is also that the
notion of a "heavenly person" can qualify God's
infinite transcendence of the world in such a way
that it follows from the logic of "being a person"
that God might not have relations with the world—
in particular, that God should not love us. This
is clearly what Tillich has in mind when he denies
it is meaningful to speak of God as "the absolute
individual"[57]—the absolute Self. "God cannot be
called a self, because the concept 'self' implies
separation from and contrast to everything which
is not self."[58] But that is impossible, for God
"participates in every life as its ground and aim.
God participates in everything that is."[59]

Another way to put this is to say that an
individual person is "external" to me. Furthermore,
as an individual being, it is perfectly conceivable
that he should remain external, not have relations
with me. It is perfectly conceivable that he
should not love me, that he should remain impassive,
as it were. But for Tillich, it is inconceivable
that God should not love us. In Tillich's view,
that is, one cannot build it into any legitimate

---

[57]ST I, p. 244.

[58]*Ibid*.

[59]ST I, p. 245.

concept of God that God might have no relations
with the world at all, however infinitely God
"transcends" the world.

It is just this sense of the personal relatedness of God which generates the fundamental
paradox that everywhere seems to accompany Tillich's
thought. For if it is intrinsic to the concept of
"God" that God utterly transcends the world, then
it is paradoxical to also insist God is "personally" related to us. Yet for Tillich the fundamental
problem is not how it is possible to assert the
former without contradicting the latter, but rather
what follows from the fact that the necessity to
assert both equally commits theology to an unresolvable paradox.

The reason it is dangerous to refer to God as
a person is not simply because one risks "losing"
God's transcendence of the world. It is also, and
equally, because doing so invites the possibility
of emphasizing God's transcendence of the world too
much. When Tillich says "God cannot be called a
self, because the concept 'self' implies separation
from and contrast to everything which is not self"[60]
it is just that sense of "separation from" which
characterizes the relation of one self to another
self that Tillich denies can characterize the nature of God's relatedness to us. Thus, Tillich's
analysis of God as the power of being inherent in
everything is meant to provide the ontological support for the thesis that it is inconceivable that

[60]ST I, p. 244.

God should be separated from us. Calling God a
person raises the possibility that God's relatedness might be something arbitrary or even withheld
from us. One might say that calling God a person
makes God "human," only all too human.

It is also this issue which lies behind Tillich's remark that it is meaningful to call God an
absolute individual "only in the sense that he can
be called the 'absolute participant.' The one term
cannot be applied without the other."[61] The God
who transcends us is always and equally the God
who "participates in everything that is."[62] God's
transcendence, therefore, must always be understood
as a transcendence in immanence—the transcendence
of a God "nearer to all creatures than they are to
themselves."[63]

Tillich's concept of God clearly requires a
unique understanding of the nature of any relatedness to God. To emphasize the radicalness of this
relation, Tillich turns the metaphor describing
the relation of two things which are "external" to
each other around, and speaks of relatedness to God
as relations which are "internal" to God:

> God as being-itself is the ground of every
> relation; in his life all relations are
> present beyond the distinctions between
> potentiality and actuality. But they are

---

[61] *Ibid.*

[62] ST I, p. 245.

[63] Tillich, *Biblical Religion and the Search
for Ultimate Reality*, p. 84.

> not the relations of God with something
> else. They are the inner relations of
> the divine life.[64]

The internality of God's relatedness to the
world is also connected with the doctrine of creation. From the concept of God as the creator of
the world it follows that whatever stands in relation to God does so only because it has "issued"
from God, who is its source and ground. But that
which is God's issue cannot stand independently of
its source; hence, the nature of relatedness to
God cannot, according to Tillich, be that of two
independent, self-subsisting entities:

> The doctrine of creation affirms that God is
> the creative ground of everything in every
> moment. In this sense there is no creature-
> ly independence from which an external rela-
> tion between God and the creature could be
> derived.[65]

The other side of the idea that God's relation to
the finite world is one in which all relations are
"internal" to the divine life is the notion that
nothing can "escape" the divine life. What Tillich
has in mind here is not only the idea that nothing
can stand, ontologically, outside the divine life
(for outside the divine life there is no being),
but also the specific claim that we cannot stand
outside of the "awareness" of that divine life.

We have seen, and discussed at greater length
elsewhere, how the idea that nothing can stand ontologically outside the divine life leads Tillich

---

[64] ST I, p. 271.

[65] *Ibid.*

to claim that God's existence cannot be discussed.

> The unapproachable character of God, or
> the impossibility of having a relation
> with him in the proper sense of the word,
> is expressed in the word 'holiness.' God
> is essentially holy, and every relation
> with him involves the consciousness that
> it is paradoxical to be related to that
> which is holy. God cannot become an ob-
> ject of knowledge or a partner in action.
> If we speak, as we must, of the ego-thou
> relation between God and man, the thou
> embraces the ego and consequently the en-
> tire relation. If it were otherwise, if
> the ego-thou relation with God was proper
> rather than symbolic, the ego could with-
> draw from the relation. But there is no
> place to which man can withdraw from the
> divine thou, because it includes the ego
> and is nearer to the ego than the ego to
> ifself. Ultimately, it is an insult to
> the divine holiness to talk about God as
> we do of objects whose existence or non-
> existence can be discussed.[66]

Remarks such as "the divine thou...includes the ego
and is nearer to the ego than the ego to itself" in
this passage express Tillich's assumption that
everyone has an intrinsic awareness of God. Now,
connecting this with what we had said in section
ii of the essay, I think it can be seen more clearly what lies behind Tillich's assumption. It is
Tillich's view that the content of awareness of God
is uniquely constituted by self-awareness. "Every
act of self-apprehension contains, as its foundation within reality, the relation to the Unconditional."[67]

---

[66]*Ibid.*

[67]Tillich, "The Conquest of the Concept of
Religion in the Philosophy of Religion," p. 139.

Insofar as Tillich's attempt to rule out the possibility of raising the question of God's existence is supported by this assumption he simply begs the question. As I have previously suggested, one cannot claim "Does God exist?" is senseless because both answers to it, affirmative or negative, are quite intelligible even granting the assumption that everyone has an awareness of God in self-awareness. At the same time, it is not obvious that Tillich's use of this assumption to characterize the unique nature of relatedness to God—where it occurs—is improper. For even if the assumption that everyone has an awareness of God is false, as it surely is, Tillich may be nevertheless quite correct in thinking that the self constitutes the content of awareness of God in those for whom it occurs. Tillich's error is in making an assumption about the purported universality of awareness of God the basis of an attempt to establish God's existence with certainty (hence, the senselessness of raising the question).

> "the certainty of the Unconditional is apprehended in self-certainty"[68]

> "the self's certainty of itself is the basis for certainty of God"[69]

> "there is no consciousness unreligious in substance"[70]

Tillich is quite justified in using the idea

---

[68] *Ibid.*

[69] *Ibid.*, p. 138.

[70] *Ibid.*, p. 139.

that we cannot "withdraw" from the divine thou in our relation to him to characterize the peculiar nature of that relation. Nevertheless, we can also see that a discussion, which begins trying to characterize the nature of God, quickly slides into a claim meant to convince us of the necessity for presupposing the existence of God. Hence, the discussion of whether God exists is "senseless" only because Tillich has allowed no possibility for that discussion.

iv

While the issue of God as an object of thought and the position which attempts to force us to presuppose God's existence are surely distinct, in Tillich's theology it is very hard to keep them separate. The God whose existence we must presuppose because God "includes" the ego is the God who stands beyond any distinction between the self and its objects of apprehension. But the God which "stands beyond the antithesis of subject and object"[71] is also the God about which "the fact that it becomes an object is indeed the primal paradox."[72] It is the God about which every statement "is necessarily in the form of paradox."[73] I think the very fact that these issues do get blended adds

---

[71]*Ibid.*, p. 123.

[72]*Ibid.*, p. 122.

[73]*Ibid.*, p. 123.

to the feeling that Tillich's paradoxes are deliberate—or at least of his own making. At the same
time, this "deliberateness" is also a result of the
particular constriction the theologian finds himself under in which, if he is to speak of God at
all, he is (a) compelled to make of God some concrete representation, some picture, yet (b) simultaneously compelled to deny that picture. It is
just this point Tillich is making when he says "in
every concern there is *something* about which one
is concerned: but this something should not appear
as a separated object..."[74] For what concerns us
ultimately is not a "something." Thus, what concerns us ultimately "cannot be a special object;
not even God..."[75] By this Tillich is not meaning
that God cannot properly be said to be what our
ultimate concern is about, but that there is nothing
"there," so to speak, which justifies our saying
that.[76] Nor could there be anything "there," for
there is nothing in what religious remarks are
about that stands outside the self as an object to
the thinking subject, and that makes them true in
the way, for example, that the person behind the
door makes it true that "someone is there."

     This is also Tillich's point in saying we

---

[74]ST I, p. 12, Tillich's emphasis.

[75]ST I, p. 14.

[76]Tillich, "The Conquest of the Concept of
Religion in the Philosophy of Religion," p. 123.

cannot "talk about God as we do of objects whose
existence or non-existence can be discussed."
Even though, when we talk about God, we must
speak of an "object," there is nothing "there"
which makes religious statements true, if they
are true. The view of the nature of religious
assertions this generates, then, is that there
can be nothing which justifies religious claims
in the way empirical evidence justifies valid
scientific assertions. The effect of this, of
course, is to appear to insulate religious claims
from criticism by making their object a private
one. Although the structure of the consciousness
of God is intrinsic to everyone, only each individual has access to any representation of the
nature of God because he is personally and unique-
present in the content of that representation.
It is important to note, at the same time, that
this insularity results from Tillich's analysis
of the nature of the "object"of religious claims,
not the willingness of the claimant to provide
support. That is, while Tillich surely numbers
among those Protestant theologians who are scepti-
cal about the possibility of there being any
"argument" for the existence of God at all, this
is not because Tillich thinks some other phenomenon (e.g., religious experience) renders argument
unnecessary, but because he thinks a proper
analysis of the concept of God renders it impossible.

Because God is not an object, but being-
itself, it is necessarily paradoxical to talk
about God in the language of physical objects.
On the other hand, it does not follow from this
that it is inconceivable that we should, nevertheless, experience God, or, as Tillich puts it, be
"grasped" by God. Thus, the sense in which the
language of physical objects is inadequate to describe our experience of God does not mean that
language is meaningless. Nor is Tillich's concept of being-itself meant to replace the language
of the "ordinary believer." Rather, Tillich's
concept of being-itself, and the restrictions
which must be put on all religious expressions,
are simply meant to force us to acknowledge that
the way in which we become aware of being-itself
is an experience for which we literally have no
"representation." But from this it does not follow that our experience of God as being-itself is
an experience of "nothing."

v

While Tillich's attempt to explicate the
concept of God is always paradoxical, often deliberately so, it is not, I have been suggesting, obviously false or meaningless. It perhaps comes
closest to being self-contradictory when, on occasion, Tillich appears to deny that whatever is
said of God is anything like what we could know
or experience. The following passage, for example, seems to go over the boundary into plain

contradiction:

> The holiness of God requires that in re-
> lation to him we leave behind the total-
> ity of finite relations and enter into a
> relation which, in the categorical sense
> of the word, is not a relation at all.
> We can bring all our relations into the
> sphere of the holy; we can consecrate the
> finite, including its internal and extern-
> al relations, through the experience of
> the holy; but to do so we must first
> transcend all relations.[77]

We can recall (from section iii) that Tillich has
been talking about the unique conditions under
which God is related to us and we to God, and he
has been trying to give sense to this uniqueness
by speaking of all relations as "internal" to
God. But now it turns out that even this relation is "not a relation at all." Granted that
theology is compelled to qualify any picture we
have of what being "related" to God is like. But
here Tillich simply seems to give with one hand
what he takes away with the other. That is, it
is one thing to alter, for some purpose, our ordinary perception of what a relation is; it is
quite another thing to say something at once "is"
relation and "is not" a relation. Moreover, the
qualifier "in the categorical sense of the word"
does not help us avoid the contradiction. At
best it is a rhetorical device to enable Tillich
to avoid making positive assertions about God at
just those points in his analysis when an apparent contradiction arises.

---

[77]ST I, p. 272.

This shift to "mystical humility" can be seen in the following passage from the same text:

> Theology, which by its nature is always in the danger of drawing God into the cognitive relation of the subject-object structure of being, should strongly point to the holiness of God and his unapproachable character in judgment of itself.[78]

On the other hand, there is another sense in which Tillich would want to admit that a picture and its qualification is "not of any use at all" and mean it straightforwardly. In many ways, it is this sense, despite its strong feel of self-contradiction, that is the most significant use of Tillich's style of paradox and negation. For this is the sense which by virtue of its flirtation with self-contradiction best illuminates the nature of the kind of concept the concept of God is. I am aware that the term "flirtation" is a somewhat gratuitous one. But if we can come to see that an apparent self-contradiction is not necessarily self-defeating, then we have grasped, in Tillich's mind, the sense in which it is meaningful to speak of paradoxes about God as "in principle unresolvable." We will have seen that it takes the radicalness of apparent self-contradiction to point beyond the realm of inadequate concrete assertions to a genuine grasping of the meaning of God. The grasping of that concept is something Tillich insists cannot be achieved "either by common sense

---

[78]*Ibid.*

or by logical thought."[79]   Rather, it is something which "calls for intuition."[80]   Its compre-
hension, more accurately, is a matter of "being
grasped."

In every theological assertion containing
a paradox of the sort Tillich says it requires
intuition to comprehend, there is an implicit attempt to describe the sense in which God is the
kind of object that cannot be an object, because
God is not in any genus—not an object of any kind.
But if God is not in any genus, then there can be
no kind of thing before our consciousness which
provides justification for our being able to speak
of God.   While theology is compelled to frame a
concept of God—and while the concept one has is
important because it determines the form one's
religiousness will take, the form for which one
is "responsible"—all the same, Tillich's whole
effort is to deny that any concept we have of God
can represent God.   And in that denial is meant
to be Tillich's view of precisely what it takes
to give meaning to the concept of God.

Since no picture can be the right one, Tillich does not suggest we replace the picture of
God as a "heavenly person" with another picture.
This is not only because Tillich thinks "heavenly
person" is all right, just as long as we acknowl-

---

[79]Tillich, "The Conquest of the Concept of
Religion in the Philosoph of Religion," p. 123.

[80]*Ibid.*

edge that it is a symbol for what we mean by God.[81] It is also because learning to understand what is meant by the use of that symbol is not a question of getting the most adequate symbol (they are all inadequate) but of coming to share the perspective from which it is said. That is what it means to call the first criterion of theology "existential."

Tillich's analysis of paradox, then, is itself the paradoxical conjunction of these two theses: in every assertion about God (1) we do have some picture before us, and (2) what we mean by God is none of those pictures. Nor is it a possibility that there could be anything there "before our consciousness" that is identical with what a thought of God is of—a picture of some fact which provides the warrant for those assertions we make.

But to say this is not the same as saying God isn't there before our consciousness. That would be going a step further than is implied by Tillich's claim that God is not a being but being-itself, beyond the distinction between essence and existence.[82] However paradoxical Tillich's concept of God is, Tillich does not retreat to silence.

---

[81]Tillich, "The Nature of Religious Language," p. 61.

[82]ST I, p. 236.

CHAPTER FIVE

INCONSISTENCY AND THE POSSIBILITY
OF THEOLOGICAL MEANING

The purpose of these essays has been not
only to sort out the causes of numerous difficulties in the thought of Paul Tillich, but also to
suggest that many of these dilemmas are simply
representative of more fundamental problems endemic to Christian theology. In particular, I have
sought to examine the logic of why certain positive assertions theologians want to, or must make
about God force them into apparent self-contradic-
tions. Thus, the issues here concern not just
Tillich but the possibility of meaning in theology
generally. The situation from which there arises
the need for Tillich to simultaneously affirm and
deny that God is a singular existing individual,
for example, generates questions beyond those per-
taining to the consistency of his own thought.
It is the possibility of doing theology under conditions of inconsistency that is itself being
raised. Yet it is precisely in this regard that
Tillich's theological writings are especially interesting: for by one means or another, Tillich's
relentless striving for inclusiveness forces the
analyst out of the comfort of that Manichaean distinction which identifies consistency with mean-

156

ingfulness and inconsistency with the necessarily
false or meaningless. It is not just a matter of
acknowledging that there may be nothing wrong,
after all, with inconsistency——i.e., that certain
forms of inconsistency may be legitimate. Rather
it is the suggestion that inconsistencies can
themselves be illuminating. And much of Tillich's
intrigue lies in the fact that he straddles both
sides of the question. Generally, Tillich is
anxious to avoid inconsistency, yet he also, sometimes, praises it.[1] Therefore, determining whether or not it makes any difference in the lives of
believers that one must simultaneously affirm and
deny God's individuality becomes a matter of dis-
covering what ranges of meaning are available
under circumstances where the possibility of
there being meaning at all is stretched to the
limit. It is, for example, only by some set of
conventions that the behavior of individuals committing certain bizarre and violent crimes is not
culpable under a system of rational law, because
it is classified as incomprehensible within it.
But this behavior is not meaningless. That is,
it does represent a range of possible human behavior——if only because human behavior includes
the possibility of acting "inhumanly."[2] It is per-

---

[1]For an interesting discussion of the question of consistency and Tillich's use of the systematic form, see Robert Schrader, *The Nature of
Theological Argument: A Study of Paul Tillich*
(Missoula, Montana: Scholars Press, 1975), Ch. IV.

[2]Today in Salt Lake City, for example, a

haps unlikely that some semantic distinction between incomprehensibility and meaninglessness
will settle theological dilemmas. But there is
surely the need for more options than presently
exist for the philosophical theologian concerned
to explicate the meaning of the Western concept
of God. Thus, in these closing remarks I would
like to explore some possibilities in one area of
this large problem: viz., can there be a conjunction of meaningful yet inconsistent claims about
God?

If certain positive assertions we make in
explication of the meaning of the concept of God
force us to assert incompatible statements about
God simultaneously, should we take that as an in-
dication that we can't really possess a concept
of God?[3] It is that holding the concept of God

---

woman threw her seven children and herself from
an eleven story window in the belief that her
husband, also having committed suicide, was the
incarnation of the Holy Trinity.

[3] The following are examples of such pairs
of incompatible assertions:

I.   (a) God wholly transcends the world
      (b) God is immanent within each of us.
II.   (a) God is not a being but is being-
          itself, part of the nature of
          everything.
      (b) God is the absolute individual.
III. (a) God does not exist.
      (b) God is existence itself.
IV.   (a) Jesus is f ly human.
      (b) Jesus is fully God (i.e., not
          human).

may be in some way self-defeating? Or is it that
the concept of God is itself contradictory? In
the last essay I gave some reasons why, even if
the answer to the former is "yes" it need not
follow that the answer to the latter is.

The difference between these two questions
corresponds roughly to a distinction that can be
made between linguistic and mental accounts of
what it is to have a concept.[4] For a linguistic
account one can turn to J. L. Austin's criterion:
"...to ask 'whether we possess a certain concept?'
is the same as to ask whether a certain word—or
rather, sentences in which it occurs—has any
meaning"[5] On a mental account, we can be said to
have some concept F if we can conceive of F—
"conceive of" entailing the occurrence of some
mental operation as thinking of or imagining F.
What this distinction emphasizes is that while it
may not be possible to give a non-paradoxical account of the mental operation of holding a concept
of God (i.e., we have no explanation of why, for
example, we can and must say God wholly transcends
the world and is also immanent within each of us),
it does not follow from this that the concept of
God is itself meaningless or unintelligible. It
is, as Tillich suggests, the word "God" which

---

[4]This is discussed by David Londey in "Concepts and God's Possibility," *Sophia*, Vol. XVLI,
No. 1, April 1978, p. 16.

[5]J. L. Austin, *Philosophical Papers* (London:
Oxford University Press, 1961), p. 12.

produces a "contradiction in the consciousness"
but this is not because the concept is incoherent.
Indeed, the ability to use the single designator
"God" in theological remarks such as the above
may give something of a clue to the nature of how
expressions using the concept God display their
meaning.

Just saying that, however, does not take us
very far in guiding a philosophico-theological
investigation seeking to establish the possibility of meaningful language about God under conditions of inconsistent assertions about him. Moreover, it is odd to be told one cannot, without
contradiction of some sort, hold the concept of
what is regarded as not only intelligible, but
supremely intelligible. (Recall Aquinas' criticism of the Pseudo-Dionysius: it is not the case
that God is unknowable or beyond all knowledge
but that God is beyond all that can be known of
him).

It is consoling, if not enlightening, to
make the historical observation that the Church
has typically resisted opting for philosophically
more consistent but theologically weaker formulations of its most important claims. Chalcedon
(451) no doubt serves as a paradigm: for in its
doctrine of the two natures—Christ is fully human yet fully God (i.e., not human)—a precedent
was set allowing for the necessity of a quite
cleanly expressed but inc: :patible pair of claims.
The necessity, in part, derives from the crucial

position of the historical conditions governing
Christian claims about God. Philosophically, it
would have been far easier to establish consistency if it were claimed only that Jesus was "like"
the Father. But the price paid for that consis-
tentcy would have indeed been severe. For the
latter claim would permit a reasonable expecta-
tion of there coming along some other historical
individual even more "like the Father" than Jesus,
and thus the position of Jesus as the unique locus
of divine revelation would be lost. Chalcedon is
also instructive in getting out another part of
the peculiar sense of "must" in the contradictori-
ness of certain claims about God—not just because
it establishes something of a tradition for theological paradox by giving it the authority of or-
thodoxy in the history of the Church, but because
it marks out a region of fundamental insolubility
within the religious life of the community. Because the exchanges surrounding Chalcedon gave
full expression to this insolubility, the Christological debates lasted longer and did not reach
the protective solutions of other (e.g., Trinitarian) early controversies. On the other hand, the
relative clarity of the discussion (in Leo's *Tome*
of 449 and the doctrine of *communicatio idiomatum,*
for example) transformed the debate into a vehicle
expressing the religious vitality of the community
and not just its intellectual shortcomings. Only
those debates reflecting diversities that genuine-
ly matter in the lives and experience of individ-

uals become the ones that do not ever really die
out.

The key for seeing the possibility of meaning within inconsistency depends upon the coincidence of a felt need for rational consistency and
the inability to have it.   In one way or another,
the question of consistency turns on a simultaneous reference to states of affairs and something
which denies them, and the situations in which
this occurs are just those where the incompatibility between what is and the opposing values seems
to be a necessary one.   Death is a universal fact
of nature, for example, yet nature perpetually
values survival.   Given this as the conditions of
our existence, the concepts of "life" and "death"
cannot co-exist.   They stalk one another; they
are in essential conflict.   In interpersonal relations, the most powerful form of necessary conflict derives from the paradox that while a pre-
requisite for all genuine love is the freedom in
which the other must be freely chosen, all the
same, there can be no love unless one is also
"compelled": i.e., unless ones freedom is captured
by the other.

In each of these cases we really do want to
rationally harmonize some striving "forced upon
our natures" with the way the world is, and in
each case we cannot succeed—not because what we
desire is logically incoherent but because the
world does not fit it.   1 is the attempt to come
to terms with experiences such as these, I am

suggesting, that lies at the bottom of the phenomenon of religious faith. But it is not simply
the conflict between "the way things are" and
"human values" that I am referring to. Rather,
it is the conflict generated by those particular
human values that are impossible to have realized
—those human values by which we strive, in a
sense, to be more than human. It is for this
reason that I describe certain desires as being
"forced upon our natures" and the conflicts they
produce as "necessary ones." For the sake of
consistency, if not otherwise, one should not
strive to deny his humanness, to transcend it;
yet it is in precisely that striving that our humanness lies. Out of this conflict that is both
within and without our nature arises the data of
religious reflection. Hence, it is an essential
religious issue to discover what it is that
forces us to hope for, to want, to strive for that
which is impossible to have. To understand how
the failure which results can be transformed into
something of beauty and meaning without inadvertently denying failure or creating substitutes for
it is at the bottom of religious sensibility. To
understand how meaning can occur precisely where
one has no reason to expect it—in the utterance
of those paradoxa the experience of essential conflict demands—is to understand what it means to
be religious. And if making those utterances
turns out to be self-defeating, then that self-
defeat must itself become a datum for religious

consciousness.

To the extent that theology has been able
to avoid either a retreat into mysticism or the
bare proclamation of the rationality of belief
through purely dogmatic systems, the genuine inconsistencies in Christian claims about man's
relation to God have been able to be a continual
source of life to the believer, rather than de-
structive of belief. For religious answers lie
not in the giving up of reason, nor in the assimi-
lation of reason to one particular (e.g., scientific) form of rationality, but in some third way
that understands the defeat of reason in the acceptance of inconsistency as one possible expression of reason. It is something of this sort, I
think, that theologians who have urged the need to do
something to reason to make room for faith have
had in mind. Perhaps unfortunately, what needs to
be "done" sometimes turns out to be not merely the
transcending of reason, but the need to kill reason, even lose one's reason. Still, to "kill reason," for example, is not to avoid reason or to
allow it to fall into disuse or to replace it with
something else, e.g., mystical union. Rather it
is to use reason to defeat itself for some higher
goal. This is an admittedly impressionistic account, and rather Hegelian sounding. But it is
one someone like Tillich would be quite comfort-
able with, since his own attitude toward reason
in faith is just this one £ using reason critic-
ally (in his case, ontological analysis) to defeat

certain forms of reason (the theological reasoning of "ordinary theism") to attain some higher
expression of faith in which the most abstract
concepts can become vehicles for the experiential
data of religion. For Tillich, what is wrong with
"theism" is that it has lost contact with the primary experiences which originally generated the
concept of God. To regain that experience, and
hence God, demands a theology attentive (in a very
Kantian way) to the paradoxa of the conditions of
any possible experience.

My interest here is less in giving an out-
line of some theory of the possibility of theological meaning under conditions of inconsistency,
than it is to give instances of the occurrence of
meaningful yet inconsistent claims. It would, in
any case, not be enough to establish some general
theory of meaning under conditions of inconsistency unless it could be shown that the particular
theological claims we have been considering in
these essays fit that theory. If the demand for
meaning is universal, then it is a demand that
must range over these particular claims. That is,
we want to be able to understand the special meaningfulness of (a) God transcends the world, and
(b) God is immanent within each of us, or of (a)
God is (b) is not a singular individual, because
theologically we must assert both.

I should say, at this point, that the possibility of turning to more poetic explanations of the
conjunction of meaning and inconsistency does not

strike me as particularly promising. The reason
for this is that the inconsistency of the pairs
of assertions above is less like, say, the inconsistency of the seas than it is like the inconsistency of something's being simultaneously red and
green all over——which is not to imply that it is
the flat inconsistency of the latter either. When
I say I am not optimistic about poetic explanations what I have in mind primarily is that one
cannot look to looseness or ambiguity to explain
assertions whose incompatibility is very much
right on the surface. However, I do not mean to
suggest that incompatibility of this strong sort
cannot be found in poetry. The *coincidentia*
oppositorum (see George Herbert's "Virtue," for
example) that the good things are the eternal/the
good things must die is a theme frequently ex-
plored in verse.

   Up to now it has been assumed the intention
of coincidental incompatible theological assertions is to express some meaning that cannot otherwise be expressed. Tillich, it was suggested, is
forced to use the language of paradox in order to
say what could not be illuminated in any other way.
But the possibility that theological incompatibles
are intended (whether or not they do) not to express meaning but rather to withold it, to mysti-
fy, cannot be ruled out. There can be the misuse
of religious language for private purposes; there
can be sheer stupidity.   ere are surely present
in the theological tradition enough smokescreens

masquerading as explanations. The Baltimore Con-
fession's answer to "What is the Trinity?" (The
Trinity is a mystery) and *Credo quia absurdam* are
prime candidates. It is significant, however,
that neither of these is an instance of a primary
theological assertion (e.g., Christ is fully God,
fully man) but rather a second-order explanation
of some primary assertion, and it seems natural
that the intention to withhold meaning should occur here. If the intention to obscure meaning
occurred in a primary assertion the implication
would be: one should stop assuming the meaning of
those assertions altogether.

While the withholding of meaning has to be
regarded as a denial of faith, it is the need for
explanation coincidental with the failure to provide it, I want to argue, that helps to produce
the pehnomenon of faith. If theology were in a
position to rationally explain those radical human needs from which religion forms, there would
be, as it were, no room for faith. But this argument may very well mean that some religious
"answers" which appear to function as explanations
are not really used for (or intended as, for that
matter) positive explanations after all (but not
as smokescreens either). It is exceedingly difficult to generalize here because only each individual is in a position to know whether, or to what
extent, he regards the claim of some religious
tradition as a positive answer for him. But what
I am suggesting is that it is often the case that

we appropriate as meaningful explanations that we
know or believe cannot explain——and we do this
because our nature forces us to seek explanations
and even explanations which fail can provide meaning and comfort.

Examples do not come easily here. But suppose we take the perplexing area of Christian
claims about survival. I will assume (but not
defend) that if (a) we do regard death as both
non-reversible and a universal empirical fact,
and (b) we also claim survival of death, then
some equivocation on "death" is entailed such
that it turns out that we do not "really" die.
Therefore, if a person believes death is universal
and non-reversible (genuine death) it is paradoxical, indeed self-defeating, but nevertheless meaningful to also believe in personal survival. "I
believe in survival, and it cannot happen (because
death is universal, etc.)." Now it has been a
standard philosophical example to regard "'I believe that p...' and 'p is not the case'" as self-
defeating and therefore meaningless. What I am
urging, however, is that in certain contexts (viz.,
religious ones) the utterance of self-defeating
assertions can be meaningful, and one reason they
can be is that they connect us with certain regions of our experience not covered by ordinary
discourse. For this reason it is perhaps better
to describe the belief in survival not as something standing over against nature but as itself
a fact of nature.

It is because these paradoxical utterances
do put us in contact with obscure but important
ranges of our experience——experiences where we
really do not know our mind about things——that
they seem "necessary" to us, something we are
forced to say no matter what we hold to be true.
One can feel such remarks capture our double-
mindedness even if they cannot dispel it. For
this reason as well, certain forms of scepticism
can be legitimately understood as religious phenomena. Not the Humean scepticism for which the
concept of a divine being is simply incoherent,
but the scepticism of someone like Camus——that
position which, although it regards the concept
of God as intelligible, finds it morally offensive
to believe in God. For Camus it is an irresolvable paradox that we exist in a world which is altogether silent to our values and to our needs.
While belief in God, Camus thinks, entails a denial of the world, we cannot shed the concept of
God altogether (as Hume thought we could). Thus
our position, religiously, is one of irremediable
despair.

I want to suggest that it is the same irresolvable paradox that produces the profound despair of scepticism that also produces the possibility of religious meaning. For the whole point
behind the sceptic's attack on religion is that
it is not as if the sceptic sees a cold and heart-
less world and the believer sees it as being all
rosey. It is the same world that is seen by both.

And if the concept of God is to function in that
world at all, it must relate to both believer and
sceptic for it to be of any possible use to either
one of them. That is, the concept can only be an
object of belief if it can also be that from which
belief can be withheld. Thus, the world silent to
our needs is, if that perception of the world is
true, the one present for the believer as well as
the sceptic, and if God is to speak to the believer it must be through that world. It is for these
sorts of reasons that we should see scepticism and
belief, faith and doubt as different sides of the
same coin, rather than two alternatives one must
choose between. This double-sidedness of faith
and doubt is something emphasized throughout Tillich's writings.

Considerable reference has been made to a
kind of necessity in the inconsistent assertions
certain regions of our experience force us to make.
It has to be made clear that the kind of necessity
in this "must" of the things "we must say" is not
logical necessity, but neither is it psychological.
It is not logical, although it often looks very
much like that when, for example, we point out
that it is "part of the grammar" of the concept of
God that we must simultaneously assert God's transcendence of the world and immanence to everything
in it. Clearly, this is an area we have only just
begun to explore——that exploration made more difficult because of our considerable confusions
about the notion of logical necessity itself. For

now, let it suffice to simply deny that the necessity is that of logical necessity on the
grounds that the reason we are forced to make
those assertions of God's transcendence and immanence simultaneously is not governed by conventions or "definitions" of the word "God" but by experience. As far as distinguishing this sense of
necessity from psychological, one can point to
the weakness of all such reductionistic accounts:
viz., that the burden of proof is on the one who
claims to be able to show that the only causes
for belief can be purely psychological ones and
that the way the world presents itself to the believer and forms the basis for his own explanation is irrelevant. At bottom, to call the necessity here psychological is not to explain belief
but rather to explain it away. In my own judgment
one might be better off to understand this necessity as simply a fact of nature rather than in
either of these two ways. At least this would
have the advantage of avoiding the feeling that
what we are dealing with is "a matter of conventions" or "merely subjective."

In warning, earlier, about the possibility
of intentional obfuscation in paradoxical assertions, I also should warn about the apparent re-
solution of them by claims about certain "illu-
sions." The incompatibility characteristic of
the sorts of assertions we have been considering
is not, in the Christian tradition at least, resolvable by explaining the incompatibility as one

of illusion and reality—i.e., where one statement expresses some apparent fact for which its
contrary turns out to be only an illusory incompatibility. One solution to the Christological
dilemma along these lines attempted to remove the
incompatibility between the two natures by claiming one to be unreal: i.e., Christ was really God
and only "appeared" as man. By rejecting Docet-
ism, and Platonic types of explanations generally,
it became clear that Christianity would take such
inconsistencies to be characteristically ones
where both statements are to be understood as
claiming facts ontologically on a par with one
another.

If poetic explanations of religious meaning
are too loose, and Platonic explanations requiring
reference to entities on one ontological level to
make sense of those on another are rejected by the
tradition, then to what area should we turn to
investigate the nature of the incompatibility in
statements expressing the theological distinction
between man and God (this distinction, as I have
suggested, is the most general form of more particular ones like that of the two natures and the
question of transcendence and immanence)? The
most promising area, it has seemed to me, is that
of interpersonal interaction. We can, and do, for
example, simultaneously love and hate the same
person. And while this might be, it is not obvious that it need be in different senses. I can
love N.N.'s power and hate the ruthlessness of

that power. But it is the same power that is the
subject of my double-mindedness. The religious
dimension of this phenomenon, that of being simultaneously captured by and repulsed by God has
been documented in Otto's *Idea of the Holy*. But
what has not been seen is how this experience, or
analogues of it, is right at hand.

It is often the case that such experiences
occur in the crises of life: e.g., I hate the one
I love when the one I love dies. But all that is
required is the coincidence of an irresolvable
need with what cannot be. I am not implying that
interpersonal relations are necessarily doomed to
failure as clearly as certain religious expecta-
tions. What I am suggesting is that the relation
of man and God is irredeemably dynamic——far more
like a contest of wills than the mystical sub-
sumption of human nature within the divine, and
that it is for this reason that the language of
paradox enters so fully into Christian theology.
Even in Christian mysticism, I would argue, this
dynamism of wills is largely retained.

While experiential interpersonal analogues
can provide a context for seeing meaningful incompatibles as more familiar, more at home than
ordinarily thought, it does not settle the fact
that we are still unable to explain how it can be
meaningful to simultaneously assert, e.g., God
transcends the world and is immanent within each
of us. Not having such explanations is not, of
course, proof that we do not understand them.

Knowing when to assert such propositions is at
least *prima facie* evidence that we do understand
them. At the same time, one must also recognize
that understanding them stretches the notion of
meaningfulness to such a limit that we risk the
distinct possibility that our assertions are not,
after all, meaningful. That is, the failure to
explain, if long lasting or pervasive enough,
even if it does not demonstrate the absence of
meaning (we really do not know how or for what the
gods of the Olympian pantheon function as explanations for the Greeks, but we can still apprehend
the presence of meaning there), can nevertheless
indicate a range of our experience where certain
expressions no longer meaningfully function. For
example, the failure of some notion of divine
anger to serve as a meaningful explanation any
longer of why there are floods is surely not a
disproof of divine activity or even of the possibility of still using predicates ascribing anger
to God. Nevertheless, it does indicate that a
range of our experience of the world has become
one where religious sensibility has, by and large,
ceased to operate. Indeed, it is the case that
natural disasters have become areas from which
the possibility of understanding them as religious
phenomena has been withdrawn. But that is a consequence, also, of the fact that religion is a
form of life—i.e., that if religion is something
that can develop and grow it can die as well.
Thus, we acknowledge that religion can cease to

apply to areas of our lives in the same way that
a culture can lose its imagination or its creativity and become stagnant and die.

In suggesting we have available areas in our
ordinary, and not so ordinary experience from
which we can draw to come to a better understanding of how there can be meaningful coincidences
of incompatible assertions, behavior, feelings,
etc., I am not for one moment assuming that this
familiarity itself provides an explanation of how
coincidental incompatibles can be meaningful. Indeed, it is beyond the scope of these remarks to
attempt anything beyond the barest hints as to
how one might go about trying to show the mecha-
nisms by which meaning under conditions of inconsistency is established.

Ordinarily, in situations where two assertions are contrary to one another, the truth of
one entails the falsity of the other. The truth
of "N.N. is dead" entails the falsity of "N.N. is
alive and well and living in Cincinnati." But
here we are faced with the dilemma that the truth
of "Jesus is God" does not entail the falsity of
"Jesus is fully man." In a sense we have even
been suggesting that one statement serves as a
necessary basis for understanding the other.

Now to give an account of how we can be said
to know this (not just meaningfully use assertions
within some context) will require, in addition to
a theological understanding of what it means to
assert those statements, an explanation of how a

claim to know can meaningfully function under
conditions in which it looks quite self-defeating
to assert it. That is, if, for whatever reason,
one must assert both that "X is red /X is green
all over," it is obviously self-defeating to assert either one. Yet it is formally, if not
materially, the same situation when one is forced
to assert "Jesus is fully human/Jesus is fully
God (i.e., not human)." If theologically one must
assert "Jesus is fully human" whenever he asserts
"Jesus is God" because it is grammatically (although not, let me again emphasize, logically) entailed by the latter that Jesus is fully man, then
it is self-defeating to assert the former as well?
Or, granting the need to maintain any inconsistency is in some sense self-defeating, is the
self-defeat that arises because we have said something meaningless? Let me propose that if the
entailment were logical then this self-defeat
would lead to incoherence. (To assert X is simultaneously red/green all over is deliberately incoherent and, therefore, either perverse or a piece
of nonsense). However, since the entailment is
not logical but experiential—or, more accurately,
grammatical: i.e., from the properties of linguistic usage based on experience—one would need some
additional reason to support the claim that the
Christological assertions are incoherent and hence
meaningless. One would be forced, that is to say,
to give a theological or   periential reason—not
just a philosophical one—to reject the meaning-

fulness of those claims.[6]

Moreover, it is not the case that it is always self-defeating to assert a claim under conditions incompatible with that claim. Let me turn,
in closing, from these instances of expressly inconsistent statements to some general considera-
tions regarding claims to know that bear on what
we have been discussing. One can often "know"
and "feel doubtful" at the same time, and here is
a quite ordinary example: You have packed your
bags and know everything is in them. But you are
also uneasy, enough to feel compelled to go back
and check through everything again. Here is
feeling uneasy, even doubtful, that is still a
case of knowing. At the moment one does go back
to check his bags, he does not know for sure perhaps, but this does not entail his not knowing.
Of course, if the doubt goes on for a long time,
then one doesn't know, but feeling uneasy or even
strongly doubtful for a time does not mean one
doesn't know. Therefore, there is no general reason to assume that feeling uneasy, having mis-
givings or doubts are not compatible with knowing:
moreover, if this is true, it is of some theological significance.

Up to this point we have been considering
statements about God that are explicitly inconsis-

---

[6] For this reason the ultimate judge of the
meaningfulness of theological assertions may have
to be the philosophical theologian rather than the
philosopher of religion.

tent. But there is also another kind of inconsistency equally as important: the implicit inconsistency of concurrent doubts in affirmations of
God. In Tillich's view, for example, there is
doubt implicit in every affirmation of divine reality.

Now while knowledge of God, with the concurrent doubts that necessarily attend those
claims, may not be the same as knowing I packed
my suitcase, with its concurrent doubts (knowing
someone's feelings would be a far better analogy,
but more complicated to work with), the point is
that "knowing a thing and doubting it" is not incompatible with knowing it because we can know
and still be of two minds about something. Worries of this sort concern claims about a class of
things we think we know or believe where our inability to clarify the distinction between real
and logical possibility is particularly trouble-
some. It is a real or only a logical possibility
that my passport is not in my suitcase if I know
I packed it? I really don't know how to answer
that question except to say we either need to get
rid of or refine the distinction. In theological
utterances this is even more crucial. It has been
a philosophical commonplace to argue you can't say
in the same breath "I believe that p...and it is
possible that not-p." But the reason you can't
say this in one breath is not because it is a
contradiction and therefo   nonsense, but rather
that by saying "possibly not p" one implies some-

thing about his position that makes the utterance
self-defeating. Yet the position in which we not
only do, but are forced to say simultaneously "*p*
and possibly not *p*" identifies what our stance is
in many religious utterances. I have mentioned
Tillich's view that there is doubt implicit in
every affirmation of divine reality. Of course
this view competes rather strongly with the claim
that God's existence is in some sense necessary,
and Tillich himself is not at all consistent
—also asserting it is not possible to doubt
the reality of being-itself. Therefore, we need
to know what kind of possibility and necessity
are involved here. Why must we say, for example,
"I believe God exists...and possibly God does not
exist"? Not only is it odd to make this doubt
explicit in such an affirmation, some (viz., Norman Malcolm) have argued that we can't say it because it is inconsistent with the conditional "If
God exists, then God necessarily exists" which is
taken as part of the meaning of the concept of
God.

My answer has been to urge that it is not so
odd, after all, to make those doubts explicit, because they are present in our experience even if
we do not voice them. It is surely painful to
have to voice them, and that might be explanation
enough for the oddness of hearing them. More important, however, I have been arguing that it is
not incoherent to express doubts coincidental with
their rival affirmations, nor does the sense of

self-defeat undeniably present here render those
utterances meaningless. To silence our doubts is
more dangerous than living with the dilemmas about
meaningfulness they produce. But to forbid religious affirmations such immediate and contravening
feelings of doubt would be to empty it of life,
or, far worse, to turn it into an ideology.

In this chapter I have tried to take a set
of problems and see what happens to them on the
borders of intelligibility—my primary justification being the perception that the possibility of
any experience of God demands coming to terms with
certain major inconsistencies in our understanding
of what the nature of our relation to God might
mean. For this reason I have also felt it necessary to investigate the possibilities of defend-
ing the idea that there can be a conjunction of
meaningful yet incompatible claims about God.

Thus, we have reached the sea again. Hope-
fully, one should have the feeling of standing at
the edge of possibilities which give promise of
the discovery of new loci for meaning in our experience. But if the feeling, at the end—at our
"return to the sea"—is that of having been once
again locked into an inexorable relationship with
ambiguity, at least one can take some satisfaction
in the fact that, more often than not, ambiguity
stems from our having too much meaning at hand
rather than too little.

APPENDIX

A NOTE ON TILLICH SCHOLARSHIP

In the stockpile of recent Tillich scholarship there is hardly anything which can, or deserves to be called the "standard" interpretation of Tillich. Rather, there have accumulated interpretations of every variety, and most scholars with an interest in rendering a consistent interpretation of Tillich's thought have been content to follow one or another of Tillich's own many leads, seeing Tillich's theology from that perspective as making some important theological or philosophical alteration to traditional Christian claims about the nature of God and man's relation to him. All that could be called "standard" then is a pervasive belief that Tillich is in some sense a "revisionist" theologian. However, there is virtually no agreement on precisely what form the nature of Tillich's revision of Christian theology takes.

To illustrate, one can identify a half dozen or so classes of interpretations of Tillich, all of which differ quite widely in their intentions and assumptions. Undoubtedly one could come up with more than the six I have chosen to recognize, but this sketch should suffice to show at least the range of diversity.

(1) First and least interesting is a class of general, expository accounts of Tillich's thought, offering no real critical interpretation of Tillich at all. Exemplary of this group are Leslie Tait's *The Promise of Paul Tillich*, Carl Armbruster's *The Vision of Paul Tillich*, Wayne Mahan's *Tillich's System*, David Kelsey's *The Fabric of Paul Tillich's Theology*, and, with the exception of his view of Tillich's Christology, George Tavard's *Paul Tillich and the Christian Message*. Armbruster's piece is fairly typical of the lot: a running summary of Tillich's thought focussing on the theme of the relation of religion and culture, there is relatively little attention to Tillich's philosophical theology. Rather, what does get close attention is an attempt to reproduce the systematic character of his theology: "the exposition strives to mirror Tillich's thought faithfully."[1] Kelsey's tendency to see Tillich as primarily a church theologian rather than as a philosopher of religion or a metaphysician is also characteristic of this group (although this is developed less as a specific thesis than it is the consequence of the lack of critical attention to Tillich's philosophical concerns). Perhaps the best that can be said for this class of commentary is that, like department store reproductions, it is relatively innocuous.

(2) A second and equally large group of

---

[1]Carl Armbruster, *The Vision of Paul Tillich*, (New York: Sheed and Ward, 1967), p. xxi.

writings on Tillich has seen Tillich as fundamentally an existentialist, or, at least, giving
an interpretation of Christian theology through
existentialist categories. One can include here
Arne Unhjem's *Dynamics of Doubt: a preface to
Tillich*, Guyton Hammond's *Man in Estrangement: a
comparison of the thought of Paul Tillich and
Erich Fromm,* David Hopper's *Tillich: a theological
portrait,* Bernard Martin's *The Existentialist Theology of Paul Tillich* (reprinted under the title
Paul Tillich's Doctrine of Man) and perhaps Kenneth Hamilton's comparison of Kierkegaard and
Tillich, *The System and the Gospel.* Hamilton's
study is highly critical of Tillich; Martin's has
the added interest of being written by a rabbi.
It is generally the case that writers in this
group come to Tillich with fairly strong philosophical and theological presuppositions of their
own. Also, since Tillich readily acknowledges the
use of existentialist anthropology in his own
understanding of the Christian message, this influence has been noted by many writers on Tillich
other than those specifically included here. I
have no particular objection to this basis for
interpreting Tillich—surely it is present in his
background. Nevertheless, it is limited by the
ability to make the categories and claims of various existentialists clear.

(3) Tillich generally regarded himself as
heir to a quasi-mystical tradition loosely associated with Augustine and the neo-Platonists, the

Franciscans and German voluntarists such as Boehme
and Schelling. John Dourley's interesting study
Paul Tillich and Bonaventure is the most systematic attempt to assess this relationship. Dourley examines Tillich's claim to stand in the
Augustinian-Franciscan tradition by using Bonaventure as a paradigm of that tradition and examining
their epistemologies of participation in God.
Dourley sees a more extensive agreement between
their religious anthropologies than even Tillich
himself explicitly allows. Although it deals with
far more than this question, another study of
Tillich which affirms his connection with this
tradition in James Luther Adams' *Paul Tillich's
Philosophy of Culture, Science and Religion*. Adams
is inclined to see Boehme as particularly influ-
ential, especially in Tillich's understanding of
religious paradox. I should mention, at this
point, that if any single work on Tillich deserves
to function as a "standard" interpretation of
Tillich, surely it is Adams', if for no other reason than that his study of Tillich is sufficiently
rich and subtle and complex that it resists the
inherent weaknesses of more single-minded interpretations. Adams' book is the kind of study one
likes to return to again and again; nevertheless,
as Adams himself admits, it is severely limited by
treating only those writings of Tillich prior to
1945. But for those inclined to see Tillich's
theological views as fund mentally consistent between earlier and later periods, it is a useful

perspective from which to view his later writings.

(4) A fourth group of Tillich commentators
sees the motivation for Tillich's re-interpretation
of the Christian message coming directly from
metaphysics, largely from the particular standpoint of Hegel's speculative system. J. Heywood
Thomas in his *Paul Tillich: An Appraisal* and his
more recent work (e.g., his address to the Tillich
Society in St. Louis, October, 1976) has been
prominent in his interest to trace connections
between Tillich and Hegel in the development of
Tillich's theology of culture. Thomas' recognition of the influence of metaphysics on Tillich's
ontology of being-itself is, of course, an issue
that all interpreters of Tillich at some point
must come to grips with: viz., Tillich's use of a
dialectic (whether Hegelian or otherwise) in his
theological method, and his understanding of the
theological question of the nature of God as a
form of the metaphysical question of being.
Robert Scharlemann's *Reflections and Doubt in the
Thought of Paul Tillich* sees Tillich as influenced
by Hegel's absolute system, but also moving signi-
ficantly beyond it by recognizing its weakness and
coming to terms with the question of how historic-
ally conditioned thought can achieve objective
certainty. For Scharlemann, Tillich's solution is
that historical thought achieves certainty not by
constructing an "absolute" whole but by responding
to the paradox of being.

(5) The fifth group of interpreters of

Tillich is by far the most radical. By taking
certain remarks of Tillich at face value, their
thesis, put most simply, is that Tillich is an
atheist. This view is alluded to briefly by
Walter Kaufmann in *The Faith of a Heretic* and
Alasdair MacIntyre in "God and the Theologians"
(*Encounter,* 21, No. 3, Sept. 1963) but is developed most fully by Leonard Wheat in *Paul Tillich's
Dialectical Humanism.* It is not so much this view,
but Wheat's presentation of it that I find flatly
outrageous. Since Wheat obviously does not take
Tillich's theology seriously, it is hard to take
Wheat seriously: "Tillich is a complete atheist
who lost his belief while completing his higher
education. Intellectually, he despises Christianity, and few doctrines have escaped his hard-worked
slur 'absurd.'"[2] In short, according to Wheat,
Tillich's *Systematic Theology* is "a broad satire
on Christian theology."[3] "Tillich's chief claim
to fame will be that he fooled a lot of people."[4]
I do not share the view that Tillich is an atheist,
but rather than argue that here, I invite the
reader to consider the arguments in this volume.

(6) The last group of Tillich studies is
the smallest (two) but clearly the most interesting and significant. Both are examinations of

---

[2]Leonard Wheat, *Paul Tillich's Dialectical
Humanism* (Baltimore: The Johns Hopkins Press,
1970), p. 187.

[3]*Ibid.,* p. 271.

[4]*Ibid.,* p. 276.

Tillich which are less interested in sorting out
the personal theological views of Tillich than in
recognizing the fact that Tillich's thought sym-
bolizes certain important philosophical-theologi-
cal problems endemic to Christian theology.
William Rowe's *Religious Symbols and God,* in addition to being an analysis of Tillich is concerned generally with the nature of religious
language and the notion of a religious symbol. It
is also one of the first studies to make a substantial use of analytic philosophy in its investigation of Tillich. Robert Schrader's *The Nature
of Theological Argument: A Study of Paul Tillich*
is interested in what difference in theology rationality makes, and, consequently, focuses both
on Tillich's explicit methodological remarks and
on Tillich's criteria for theological assertions
in his own arguments. For those inclined to think
Tillich is part of a Protestant tradition resistant to rationality in theology, it is interesting
that Schrader argues Tillich is not only rational
but attempts to be rational in the highest degree.

I do not feel it is my position to attempt
to locate my own work amidst this or any other
classification of Tillich scholarship. As I indicated in the introduction, my goal has been to
develop analyses and arguments that should be able
to stand or fall on their own. Moreover, it is
not the purpose of this book to refute other existing interpretations. Nevertheless, my interpretation of Tillich differs from those in at
least one important respect: I do not interpret

Tillich as a revisionist theologian, but as a theologian who is constantly attempting to maintain
traditional Christian claims about God.

I have suggested that most interpretations
of Tillich see Tillich as making one or another
philosophical or theological revision of certain
classical Christian claims. One of the more obvious is Tillich's apparent denial that God is a
singular existing individual. Interpreters of
Tillich have seen the motives for this deriving
from outside the domain of Christian theology—
from existentialism, from metaphysics, etc. However, I do not see Tillich as a revisionist theologian, and certainly not one motivated by interests external to Christian theology (although he
obviously has interests beyond Christian theology).
For that reason, my own understanding of Tillich
becomes, itself, a revisionist interpretation.
Why? I am convinced Tillich is operating fundamentally as a classical Christian theologian,
making an attempt to affirm traditional Christian
claims about God and our relation to him, and that
his use of a quasi-Hegelian dialectic, the categories of existentialism, a version of Platonic
ontology and so forth is simply a set of inputs
that are overlaid on Tillich's primary concerns,
which are not to try to write a Christian philosophy of "being" but to use ontological, philosophical, mystical and existential categories—whatever is available to him— ᴏ elucidate certain
fundamental tensions and paradoxes Tillich feels

are intrinsic to Christian theology, in particular to the concept of God. As I try to demonstrate
in the essay "God and Singular Existence," for
example, Tillich does not flatly or unequivocally
deny that God is a being, but is forced to assert
two incompatible claims about God simultaneously.
God is/is not a being. The reasons why Tillich is
forced into such apparent contradictions is precisely why I find Tillich interesting as a theologian. And this leads me to the second respect
in which I might try to characterize my own interpretation of Tillich. My interest in Tillich is
because I see his theology reflective of certain
problems that are important to philosophical theology. That is, it is not terribly important to
determine whether or not Tillich was himself an
atheist. But it is important to determine why an
atheism of some sort may be a possible position
within Christian theology, and not simply an al-
ternative to it. What that sort of atheism is,
and how it derives from the attempt to make certain positive assertions about God has been one
consideration of this volume.

     In sum, what I am offering is a revisionist
understanding of Tillich's theology insofar as I
see Tillich's thought as not a revision of but
clearly within the classic tradition of Christian
theology, and in particular, as I have argued, considerably closer to the theology of Thomas Aquinas
than is often realized.

SELECTED BIBLIOGRAPHY

I. WORKS BY PAUL TILLICH

Tillich, Paul. *Biblical Religion and the Search for Ultimate Reality*. Phoenix Books. Chicago: The University of Chicago Press, 1964.

_____. *Dynamics of Faith*. Harper Torchbooks. New York: Harper and Row, Publishers, 1957.

_____. "Escape from God." *The Shaking of the Foundations*. New York: Charles Scribner's Sons, 1948.

_____. "Existential Philosophy: Its Historical Meaning." *Theology of Culture*. Edited by Robert C. Kimball. A Galaxy Book. New York: Oxford University Press, 1964.

_____. "God's Pursuit of Man." *The Eternal Now*. London: SCM Press, 1963.

_____. "In Everything Give Thanks." *The Eternal Now*. London: SCM Press, 1963.

_____. "Natural and Revealed Religion." *Christendom*. Vol. I, No. 1 (Autumn, 1935), 159-70.

_____. "Philosophy and Theology." *Religion in Life*. Vol. X, No. 1 (winter, 1941), 21-30.

_____. *Religiöse Verwirklichung*. Berlin: Furche, 1929.

_____. *Systematic Theology*. 3 vols. Chicago: University of Chicago Press, 1951-63.

_____. "The Concept of God." *Perspective*, Vol. II, No. 3 (January, 1950), 12.

_____. "The Conquest of the Concept of Religion in the Philosophy of Religion." *What is Religion?* Edited by James Luther Adams. New York: Harper & Row, Publishers, 1969.

_____. *The Courage To Be.* A Yale Paperbound. New Haven: Yale University Press, 1952.

_____. "The Divine Name." *The Eternal Now.* London: SCM Press, 1963.

_____. "The Idea of God as Affected by Modern Knowledge." *Crane Review,* Vol. I, No. 3 (Spring, 1959), 83-90.

_____. "The Idea of the Personal God." *Union Review,* II, No. 1 (November, 1940), 8-10. Reprinted as "Science and Theology: A Discussion with Einstein." *Theology of Culture.* Edited by Robert C. Kimball. A Galaxy Book. New York: Oxford University Press, 1964.

_____. *The Interpretation of History.* Translated by N. A. Razetski and Elsa L. Talmey. New York: Charles Scribner's Sons, 1936.

_____. "The Meaning and Justification of Religious Symbols." *Religious Experience and Truth.* Edited by Sidney Hook. New York: New York University Press, 1961.

_____. "The Nature of Religious Language." *Theology of Culture.* Edited by Robert C. Kimball. A Galaxy Book. New York: Oxford University Press, 1964.

_____. "The Philosophy of Religion." *What Is Religion?* Edited by James Luther Adams. New York: Harper & Row, Publishers, 1969.

_____. "The Religious Symbol." *Daedalus,* Vol. 87, No. 3 (1958), 1-21.

_____. *The Theology of Paul Tillich.* Edited by Charles W. Kegley and Robert W. Bretall. New York: The Macmillan Company, 1956.

_____. "The Two Types of Philosophy of Reli-
gion." *Theology of Culture*. Edited by
Robert C. Kimball. A Galaxy Book. New York:
Oxford University Press, 1964.

_____. "Ueber die Idee einer Theologie der
Kultur." *Religionsphilosophie der Kultur:
Zwei Entwürfe von Gustav Radbruch und Paul
Tillich*. Berlin: Reuther and Reichard, 1919.

_____. *Ultimate Concern*. Edited by D. Macken-
zie Brown. Harper Colophon Books. New York:
Harper & Row, Publishers, 1965.

II. OTHER WORKS

Adams, James Luther. *Paul Tillich's Philosophy of
Culture, Science, and Religion*. New York:
Schocken Books, 1970.

Armbruster, Carl. *The Vision of Paul Tillich*.
New York: Sheed and Ward, 1967.

Brown, Patterson. "St. Thomas' Doctrine of Necessary Being." *Aquinas: A Collection of Critical Essays*. Edited by Anthony Kenny. Anchor
Books. Garden City, New York: Doubleday &
Company, Inc., 1969.

Brown, Stuart C. *Do Religious Claims Make Sense?*
New York: The Macmillan Company, 1969.

Cameron, Bruce. "The Hegelian Christology of Paul
Tillich." *Scottish Journal of Theology*, 29,
No. 1 (1976), 27-48.

Cartwright, Richard L. "Negative Existentials."
Philosophy and Ordinary Language. Edited
by Charles E. Caton. Illini Books. Urbana:
University of Illinois Press, 1963.

Cell, Edward. *Language, Existence, and God*.
Nashville: Abingdon Press, 1971.

Dourley, John. *Paul Tillich and Bonaventure*.

194 The Non-Existence of God

Leiden: Brill, 1975.

Fisher, James V. "Tillich's Early Use of 'Gestalt' and Its Implications for the Meaning of Meaning." *AAR Philosophy of Religion and Theology Program* (1976), 265-284.

Ford, Lewis S. "Tillich and Thomas: The Analogy of Being." *The Journal of Religion*, XLVI, No. 2 (April, 1966), 229-245.

_____. "The Appropriation of Dynamics and Form for Tillich's God." *Harvard Theological Review*, 68 (January, 1975), 35-51.

_____. "Tillich's Implicit Natural Theology." *Scottish Journal of Theology*, 24 (August, 1971), 257-270.

Gill, Jerry H. "Paul Tillich's Religious Epistemology." *Religious Studies*, 3 (1967), 477-498.

Hall, Theodore. *Paul Tillich's Appraisal of St. Thomas' Teaching on the Act of Faith*. Rome: Catholic Book Agency, 1968.

Hamilton, Kenneth. *The System and the Gospel: A Critique of Paul Tillich*. Grand Rapids: Eerdmans, 1967.

Hammond, Guyton B. *Man in Estrangement: a comparison of the thought of Paul Tillich and Erich Fromm*. Nashville: Vanderbilt University Press, 1965.

Heidegger, Martin. *Being and Time*. Translated by John Macquarrie and Edward Robinson. New York: Harper & Row, Publishers, 1962.

Hook, Sidney. *The Quest for Being*. A Delta Book. New York: Dell Publishing Co., Ind., 1961.

Hopper, David. *Tillich: a theological portrait*. Philadelphia: J. B. Lippincott, 1968.

Kaufmann, Walter. *The Faith of a Heretic*. Garden City, N.Y.: Doubleday & Company, 1961.

Keefe, Donald J. *Thomism and the Ontological Theology of Paul Tillich*. Leiden: Brill, 1971.

Kelsey, David. *The Fabric of Paul Tillich's Theology*. New Haven: Yale University Press, 1967.

Kenny, Anthony. *Descartes*. New York: Random House, 1968.

_____. *The Five Ways*. New York: Schocken Books, 1969.

Kierkegaard, Soren. *Concluding Unscientific Postscript*. Translated by David F. Swenson and Walter Lowrie. Princeton: Princeton University Press, 1941.

MacIntyre, Alisdair. "God and the Theologians." *Encounter*, 21, No. 3 (September, 1963).

MacLeod, Alistair M. *Paul Tillich: an essay on the role of ontology in his philosophical theology*. London: Allen & Unwin, 1973.

McClean, George. *Man's Knowledge of God According to Paul Tillich: A Thomistic Critique*. Washington, D.C.: Catholic University of America Press, 1958.

Mahan, Wayne. *Tillich's System*. San Antonio: Trinity University Press, 1974.

Malcolm, Norman. "Anselm's Ontological Arguments." *The Philosophical Review*, LXIX, No. 1 (January, 1960) 41-62. Reprinted in *The Many-Faced Argument*. Edited by John H. Hick and Arthur C. McGill. New York: The Macmillan Company, 1967, pp. 301-320.

Martin, Bernard. *The Existentialist Theology of Paul Tillich*. New York: Bookman Associates, 1963.

O'Meara, Thomas F. "Tillich and Heidegger: A
        Structural Relationship." *Harvard Theologi-
        cal Review,* LXI (April, 1968), 249-261.

_____, and Weisser, Donald M., eds. *Paul
        Tillich and Catholic Thought.* Rev. ed.
        Garden City, N.Y.: Image Books, 1969.

Owen, G. E. L. "Plato on Not-Being." *Plato: A
        Collection of Critical Essays.* Vol. I. Ed-
        ited by Gregory Vlastos. Anchor Books.
        Garden City, N.Y.: Doubleday & Company, Inc.,
        1970.

Quine, Willard Van Orman. "On What There is."
        From a Logical Point of View. 2d. ed. Har-
        per Torchbooks. New York: Harper & Row,
        Publishers, 1963.

Robertson, John C. "Tillich's 'Two Types' and
        the Transcendental Method." *Journal of Re-
        ligion,* 55 (April, 1975), 199-219.

Ross, Robert R. N. "Tillich and Plato." *Sophia,*
        XV, No. 3 (October, 1976), 26-29.

_____. "Hegel, Tillich and the Theology of
        Culture." *Kairos and Logos.* Edited by John
        J. Carey. Proceedings of North American Paul
        Tillich Society (forthcoming).

Rowe, William L. *Religious Symbols and God.* Chi-
        cago: The University of Chicago Press, 1968.

Russell, Bertrand. *The Principles of Mathematics.*
        2d. ed. New York: W. W. Norton & Co., 1937.

Santoni, R. E. "Symbolism and Ultimate Concern:
        A Problem." *Anglican Theological Review,* 49
        (January, 1967), 90-94.

Scharlemann, Robert P. *Reflection and Doubt in
        the Thought of Paul Tillich.* New Haven: Yale
        University Press, 1969.

Schrader, Robert W. *The Nature of Theological*

  Argument: A Study of Paul Tillich.   Missoula,
  Montana: Scholars Press, 1975.

Schwanz, P.   "Plotin und Tillich."   *Kairos*, 14,
  No. 2 (1972), 137-141.

Shaffer, Jerome.   "Existence, Predication and the
  Ontological Argument."   *The Many-Faced Argument. (op. cit.)*

Strawson, P. F.   *The Bounds of Sense: An Essay on
  Kant's "Critique of Pure Reason."*   London:
  Methuen & Co. Ltd., 1966.

Tait, Leslie.   *The Promise of Paul Tillich.*   Philadelphia: J. B. Lippincott, 1971.

Tavard, George.   *Paul Tillich and the Christian
  Message.*   New York: Scribners, 1962.

Thomas, John Heywood.   *Paul Tillich: An Appraisal.*
  Richmond, Virginia: John Knox Press, 1966.

Unhjem, Arne.   *Dynamics of a Doubt: A Preface to
  Tillich.*   Philadelphia: Fortress Press, 1966.

Urban, William M.   "A Critique of Professor Tillich's Theory of the Religious Symbol."
  The Journal of Liberal Religion, 2 (Summer,
  1940), 34-36.

Wainwright, W. J.   "Paul Tillich and Arguments
  for the Existence of God."   *Journal of the
  American Academy of Religion,* 39 (June, 1971),
  171-185.

Wedberg, Anders.   *Plato's Philosophy of Mathematics.*   Stockholm: Almquist and Wicksell,
  1955.   Chapter III reprinted in   *Plato: A
  Collection of Critical Essays.*   Vol. I.
  (op. cit.)

Wheat, Leonard.   *Paul Tillich's Dialectical Humanism: Unmasking the God above God.*   Baltimore:
  The Johns Hopkins Press, 1970.

Williamson, C. M.   "Tillich's Two Types of Philosophy of Religion: A Reconsideration."   *Journal of Religion,* 52 (July, 1972), 205-222.

Cover photograph by

Susan Ross